EDUCATIONAL LEADERSHIP FOR THE TWENTY-FIRST CENTURY

BUILDING A CAPACITY FOR CHANGE

PETER J. ZSEBIK, Ph.D.

iUniverse, Inc.
Bloomington

Educational Leadership for the Twenty-First Century
Building a Capacity for Change

iUniverse books may be ordered through booksellers or by contacting:

iUniverse
1663 Liberty Drive
Bloomington, IN 47403
www.iuniverse.com
1-800-Authors (1-800-288-4677)

Because of the dynamic nature of the Internet, any Web addresses or links contained in this book may have changed since publication and may no longer be valid.

ISBN: 978-1-4502-5926-2 (sc)
ISBN: 978-1-4502-5927-9 (ebk)

Printed in the United States of America

iUniverse rev. date: 2/1/2011

CONTENTS

FOREWORD
BY LEWIS FRIED

Having spent the last quarter century as a secondary school and university educator, department head, and curriculum writer and leader, I have been a first-hand witness to the one constant in the public education system: change. And heading into the start of my fourth decade in education, I am keenly aware of how vital this work-in-progress is to our collective success in the future.

It seems that from the very beginnings of public education as we know it, each generation has bemoaned the 'crisis' in education undoubtedly caused by the shortcomings of the 'younger generation,' and the related 'crises' are rooted in the central social, political, and cultural ideologies of a particular time and place. It is rare, then, that we come across an approach that addresses these issues in a manner which philosophically engages them and simultaneously offers a clear-headed combination of analysis and 'meta'-synthesis. Somehow, Peter Zsebik has managed to do just that.

Part of what allows Zsebik to accomplish this difficult feat is rooted in the fact that he recognizes and works from the 'non-position' Jacques Derrida puts forward in his (in)famously aphoristic (and remarkably mis-interpreted) axiom, "there is nothing outside the text." Zsebik's analysis uses deconstruction in its greatest strength; namely, that deconstruction recognizes that no institution can exist outside the social and cultural influences of authority, supremacy, and opposition. As the range of those who are considered educational leaders (and experts) continues to widen, growing from the traditional quartet of teachers, boards of education, religious leaders, and government bureaucrats/ministries, to a much wider group of stakeholder-participants, including parents, students, business leaders, economists, psychologists/psychiatrists, sociologists, neurologists, pharmacologists, technology gurus, futurists, and beyond, the level of conflict and convolution has only increased. Zsebik's greatest strength is that he is able to identify the key issues and ideas in his analysis, allowing him to outline both the strengths and weaknesses of the current system without blindly supporting any single approach.

What Zsebik 'sees' is the postmodern world, with all its challenges. Postmodernism, having abandoned the comforts of a meaningful "grand narrative" and the belief in traditional concepts of truth and knowledge in favour of "micro-narratives" and a world wherein " . . . the old poles of attraction represented by nation-states, parties, professions, institutions, and historical traditions are losing their attraction," requires nothing if not a total re-examination of both educational theory and practice. This is no small task, and this book rises to the occasion precisely by recognizing that the postmodern world poses enormous challenges in terms of educational leadership. Zsebik's semiogically-focused concept of "SPACE" identifies the "elements of a school environment" need to create a new vision of the traditional power structures within learning institutions. As importantly, Zsebik has found an way to re-think the concept of "ethos" as it applies to education. Zsebik's own analysis discovers unity in uniqueness, in the interplay between the highly localized nature of the individual educational institution and his insightful explanation of "international education," which would assist "students to internalize the connections between themselves, as individuals, and the rest of the world."

The movement of Zsebik's analysis leads him to identify that despite the rear-guard battle of modernism to hold the educational fort, educational theory and practice must adapt itself to the postmodern condition. Significantly, Zsebik does not see this struggle as an either/or; instead, he perfectly summarizes one of Jean François Lyotard's most important ideas:

> Postmodernity is not a new age, but the rewriting of
> some of the features claimed by modernity, and first
> of all modernity's claim to ground its legitimacy on
> the project of liberating humanity as a whole through
> science and technology. But as I have said, that rewriting
> has been at work, for a long time now, in modernity
> itself.

Zsebik rightly identifies the most appropriate reaction to postmodern change is not simply to completely abandon the past. Instead, by invoking a model of first- and second-order change processes, he clearly opts for a methodology which can, at the very least, help determine the conditions for adapting to "the sociopolitical changes in which the system is embroiled," and at very best would allow educators and educational leaders to recognize one of Foucault's most prescient notions: "ideas are more active, stronger, more resistant, more passionate than "politicians" think. . . . But it is because the world has ideas (and because it constantly produces them) that it is not passively ruled by those who are its leaders or those who would like to teach it, once and for all, what it must think."

Here then within these pages you will find a blueprint for all educators who are interested in making a change to their educational environment; one that may prove fruitful for the coming years as mass education undertakes to overcome its biggest challenges yet. Quite clearly, our best hope for the future lies in the passion and commitment of educators and educational leaders such as Peter Zsebik.

Lewis Fried
Adjunct Instructor, Queen's University Faculty of Education

INTRODUCTION

Early in my career, I was given the privilege to teach and work in different parts of the world. During this time, I used different curricular programs, and I taught children from totally different cultures. Coming from a small town, these times in my life opened up a whole new world of understanding and experience. And I loved every minute of it. In fact, the complexity of the educational environment was such that I felt compelled to learn as much as I could, and this I undertook not only within an academic environment, but also in my daily life experiences. In fact, I was so immersed in the expatriate lifestyle as an educator, I fully expected once I returned to public education that it would feel like putting on an old glove—comfortable, known, and familiar.

Instead, what I found is that the educational environment I knew twenty years ago, that "old glove" of public education, no longer seemed to be able to do the job; it felt constrictive, there were holes in the "fingers," and the body was wearing thin to the point that if I looked closely I could see through the fabric of purpose and direction.

As a matter of fact, while I was away, and since my return from overseas, huge shifts in social patterns had occurred, and they have not let up. New ways of interacting with people and information via the evolving communications technology, changing immigration patterns, and declining birth rates (at least in western countries) have placed enormous pressures on individuals in these societies to understand these sweeping changes and to use them to their best advantage.

In contrast, public education, once a system designed primarily to prepare students to work and live in the society they will inherit, may now be feeling its age. Designed and instituted more than one hundred years ago, this socializing structure has attempted to stay relevant to the society it is serving. Now, however, it can be argued with relative ease that the complexity of our society is surpassing the abilities of our education system to address this complexity. Granted, public education has been consistent in its attempt to address these changes in society, but oftentimes these attempts end up being temporary measures or even bandage-like solutions.

This is not to say that good things are not happening in public education. In fact, it may be that the reason for these success stories is because of the words we use to describe these success stories—radical, innovative, unconventional, etc. In point of fact, there are success stories everywhere, and this is where we must look.

School leaders who have incorporated fundamental changes in their educational environment do not do it alone. They always seek support from their community, and together in teams they have taken it on themselves to affect change; radical change that explores the very notion of a school's purpose in relation to their contemporary society. In effect they have turned the school upside down and have created a different learning community from the bottom up where all parties in that community contribute to that shared understanding. They have created a culture, or **ethos,** that makes that school unique and inspiring. They have built a capacity for change.

How these success stories and innovations begin is by asking questions. It is by taking the step to engage the entire school community in ongoing discussions and shared understandings. It is by exploring the needs and challenges of the community which the school is servicing. It is by letting go of past traditions and understandings of what constitutes a school, and allowing ongoing innovation from other sources and parties to enhance the different learning environments. In effect, it is allowing the village to teach the child.

It is only in this way that we can peer into the educational looking glass to see what positive attributes should be kept within the school environment and what changes could be made for change that would benefit the whole school community.

The book can divided into three common areas of discourse. A broader understanding of these areas will provide one with a complete picture for building a capacity for change appropriate for the twenty-first century.

The first eleven chapters focus primarily on the state of the educational environment and its different elements. Much time is spent on this area as it is imperative that if any change is to occur, then a full understanding of the past be known to help frame the future. It is hoped that a **deconstruction** of this nature will help to clarify and organize one's own understanding of the public education environment as a traditional social construct—its origins, its development, and its current status in the public domain. This includes the different influences that have been placed on education, particularly current social and political influences.

The next three chapters of the book focus primarily on the curriculum, particularly the nature of a curriculum, the motivations that drive it, and how it is used in school settings to create the social and political ethos of a school environment. This area is felt also to be of great import for it is only with an understanding of the social and political nature of the community that we are able to affect any change felt necessary.

The last two chapters attempt to provide new directions for public education as a framework for change. These new directions are a direct result of current research and trends in education that have the capacity to affect change in the social environment.

At the end of each chapter you will find discussion questions that can be used for individual reflection or for group reflection. These questions will provide opportunity for workshop leaders and faculty to help focus on the issues being raised in the book, and to provide an incentive for further research and development.

Passion is an essential ingredient for this book. Passion is also an essential ingredient for educators, be they at the front of the classroom, in the office, or working as senior level administration. Passion is all we need for the education community to undertake a seemingly insurmountable task and approach it from a different direction that is more compatible with today's society. The students we are charged with educating can realize their full potential within their society as a responsible generation of adults only if we can prepare them for the busy world of tomorrow, and for that one needs passion.

Certain words have been highlighted when they have been used for the first time in the book. The highlighting indicates that definitions for these words can be found in the glossary at the back to enhance your reading experience.

Here then is the beginning of the journey.

CHAPTER 1

SETTING THE STAGE

An old Chinese proverb expresses the wish that one may live in interesting times. Indeed, if there was ever a time for this saying to ring true, it is now, at the beginning of the twenty-first century, when our increasing reliance on technology fuels the interest of our times. From e-mail to Twitter, current technology provides contemporary society with instant access to information, unparalleled in the history of mankind.

As information technology evolves within our culture, it continues to challenge traditional ways of delivering information. History is rife with precedent-setting shifts in which a faster movement of knowledge and information drive technological and cultural change. The following examples demonstrate the evolution of technological change:

1. Due to the advent of printing press technology in the late-fifteenth century, the Catholic Church lost its monopoly on interpreting the Christian religion.
2. Motorized technology replaced traditional cavalry in the mid-twentieth century
3. Motion picture and television media technology replaced vaudeville and parlor entertainment, also in the mid-twentieth century
4. The telephone and Internet communication technology replaced a large number of traditional letters and correspondence at the end of the twentieth century

These enormous changes in technology have already impacted western society's communication processes, and in the process have also blurred the customary distinctions between work and leisure time. It also appears that the individual's new opportunity to dialogue on any chosen subject without restriction (on forums such as Twitter) is challenging the established media. By extension, this also means that the "message" these new media are conveying is that unlimited access to information is the number one imperative of society.

In contemporary society, not only is an individual able to react to events without the aid of traditional media sources, but thanks to available technology, that individual can now access a whole new pattern of information distribution. The effect of this development is akin in scope to the historical references cited above. As a result, this free flow of information heralds a new era of technologically-aided social interaction.

This unrestricted access, while politically appropriate, poses unique challenges for mass education: How do we acknowledge these social changes within the relatively static culture of education? Why do our current educational frameworks no longer appear to fully address the needs of our contemporary society?

These questions do not negate the whole education system; there are still many areas that remain valid and can be considered as dogmas, or essential elements, needed to maintain the public education system. These areas include the following:

- Maintaining political and academic credibility (e.g. curriculum, professional development that is in line with current social trends) by interpreting information and ideas and allowing them to flow
- Using regulatory bodies such as government, boards, and teacher's unions to define and maintain political structures and policy.

The point, however, is that these educational dogmas have reached their prime; they are slowly losing their authority to the burdens that society places on education. In other words, many educational strategies are showing their age.

The current approach to establishing new educational directions has been as ineffective as trying to use a bandage to keep a severed arm from falling off. System-wide challenges often occur because policy and academic orientations in public education still adhere to century-old notions of system organization. These notions appear more irrelevant with each passing day. The academic world has made several attempts to determine different ways of addressing these issues. These attempts range from creating new curricula and methods, to paralleling complexity theory, discussed in Chapter 2, with the academic environment (Fullan 2003). Regardless of the theories of organization being discussed, however, the overall system organization that encourages top-down decision making and labor-intensive, results-driven processes is still in place.

To put it plainly, the educational conventions that currently define mass education are no longer in sync with today's social conventions. In fact, public education is a historically referenced model of organization; it was established chiefly during the nineteenth-century industrial and twentieth-century modernist periods, and its goal was to respond to the existing social needs of that time. Furthermore, most educational development over that time span was due to some technological modification that encouraged a sense of progressivism. And yet we still find teachers who use teaching techniques, technologies, and methodologies that would be familiar even to those who retired twenty years previously. In fact, if we were to hypothetically resurrect a teacher who retired fifty years ago, it is likely that there would be very little need to explain to that teacher how things work in the twenty-first century classroom, with perhaps some technological exceptions. Regardless, that resurrected teacher would almost immediately be comfortable working in the classroom once more.

And yet, so much has happened on so many different levels in our society that we are all left pondering the nature of our profession. We still find questions that beg a response:

- Is mass education purely a stabilizing force within the fabric of our society?

- Is its sole purpose to check progress?
- Will mass education's inability to affect change eventually spell its demise as a socializing instrument for our world?

Often when one is confronted by an institutional environment, one is left with little choice but to accept it as an acknowledged entity worthy of its position. If that entity is attached to a long history, then full acceptance requires very little effort. Indeed, it appears that in today's postmodernist environment, very little is needed to validate an institution and its mandated value system; slick marketing and the creation of a perceived need for the product being marketed. In short, the postmodernism age has allowed a number of distractions to enter the public consciousness, but there is very little critical dialogue in the academic environment that addresses these concerns.

It is also important to note that mass education can be termed a ***metalinguistic,*** or language-oriented, phenomenon. Indeed, if education were to adhere to the same frameworks as language, then in order for education to maintain its relevancy, a new vocabulary and grammar (espoused by thinkers ranging from Levi-Strauss to Barthes) would need to be constructed. Utilizing this philosophical focus could allow for a process-oriented development to help to generate new directions. Contemporaries such as Waters, Marzano, et al., espouse systemic notions of what they call second-order change. Second order change will be given a more complete explanation in Chapter 15, but briefly it is a notion borrowed from physics that implies decision making as a more organic process, as opposed to the more traditional linear thinking and decision making processes that appear currently in place. In every case, these researchers give evidence that this concept is not new, and may ultimately provide a direction for education which addresses the inconsistencies between mass education and contemporary society. With this in mind, we can now undertake a more complete exploration of mass education.

The following pages attempt to shed light on the implications and insights that come to the forefront when treating mass education as an extension of our society. These historical, physical, and social concepts are recognized parts of the educational environment; they have been identified as useful in the deconstruction process. We will also discuss how this treatment can provide new insight into future directions for mass education by exploring a number of theoretical and practical concepts.

A discussion this grandiose in nature requires some background, so we will begin with a brief overview of the nature of mass or public education, including both historical and contemporary influences that have direct implications on the educational environment. Once this framework is established, we will proceed to a discussion of the notion of a second-order change **paradigm**. These paradigms could provide a more effective platform that would make public education more relevant, therefore enhancing its impact on our society.

In these pages begins a new way of thinking; one that will provide academic leaders with the insight, inspiration, and creative thinking necessary to bring mass education in line with the challenges and opportunities of twenty-first century.

A Reminder about the Discussion Questions

Throughout the book, each chapter will end with discussion questions that can facilitate individual study or group discussions, depending on the nature of the academic context. Please see these questions/prompts only as guidelines from which to begin your enquiry.

Remember, there are no right or wrong answers—only answers that can be supported by theoretical and practical development through a critical-thinking process.

DISCUSSION AND REVIEW QUESTIONS FOR CHAPTER 1

1. What are some of the social issues currently confronting today's society?

2. Define the following terms. Once you have made the attempt, please see glossary at the back of the book to check your answers:
    a. Sociopolitical
    b. Sociohistorical
    c. Metanarrative
    d. Metalinguistic
    e. Postmodern

3. What is meant by education being a historically referenced model?

4. Explore more fully the notion that education is a metalinguistic narrative. What is meant by this term? Do you agree?

5. With reference to issues found in Chapter 1, discuss how you see these issues impacting public education.

6. With reference to your own experiences as an educator, discuss and outline other issues that you see as impacting public education.

7. Develop a comprehensive diagram (i.e. mind map) outlining any connections you find in your answers. Discuss any ramifications that come to light.

CHAPTER 2

EXPLORING THE CURRENT SYSTEM OF PUBLIC EDUCATION

The concept of mass education has been with us for some time, and yet the way it's evolved has led to a less-than-satisfactory educational environment for today's needs. There is evidence of this sense of disenchantment, not only around the staff room, but also within a good deal of the scholarly literature available—literature that espouses the need for change to the current academic environment.

For instance, in his relatively recent book, *Change Forces with a Vengeance* (2003), Fullan details a number of underlying concepts that relate to changing the nature of education. This is the third in a series of books in Michael Fullan's chaos theory trilogy. This series explores notions that are uncovered when chaos theory (or complexity theory, as he calls it) is applied to education. He attempts to show how complexity theory has pushed the envelope further by providing new insights and lessons about changes in education. These include the need for a moral purpose to create a focus and the need for what Fullan calls tri-level reform at

- the school and community level
- the local district level
- the state level

Fullan further states that in order for any change to occur, it should start at the top of the educational structure and then trickle down. He understands the many dangers of too much or too little change; the end result of either extreme could be that nothing changes because the "prescription" was not appropriate for that system. He believes that systems therefore must be guided, not managed, for it is with management that things deteriorate. In contrast, he believes that social systems, such as that found within an educational context, have a seeming life of their own, where growth, development, and change occurs naturally within the system dynamic. Effectively guiding any positive initiatives within this context to best enhance the whole organization is the only question still on the table (Fullan 2003).

Interestingly, however, while works such as Fullan's sheds positive light on a number of issues facing education today, they appear to be almost bandage-like in their perspective: much of the focus for change centers on the current system structure—in Fullan's example, by investing in more informed leadership. And so how can education remain pertinent in the face of twenty-first-century challenges?

It is also interesting to note that Fullan appreciates the need for educational discourse to be rooted in chaos (or complexity) theory. I concur on this aspect for the simple reason that the educational environment has become so convoluted, perhaps because of the nature of our twenty-first-century society. But if that is the case, then a move such as the one cited above would require a level of perception in our education system not yet attained in the wider public consciousness.

To a large extent, Fullan is right. Anyone who is in education can see that the complexity of mass education has risen dramatically. In order to properly identify and explain its current features, we will need a solid understanding of complexity theory.

Having said that, however, one could speculate the issues and challenges facing public or mass education are rooted much more deeply than expected. This means that analyzing complexity theory may not prove sufficient to understand how mass education has evolved, and then to render it more pertinent to the complex needs of contemporary society.

One of the problems that may stymie this process is the fact that the politics governing mass education attempt to please all people all the time.

This can be evidenced by the broad swath of curricular foci currently found in the western world's educational systems. As educators, we end up trying to react to occurrences that take place outside the classroom by incorporating new items into our classrooms. A typical example is the use of the latest technological wizardry. This technological emphasis is not a bad thing, unless it creates an environment where we lose the overall educational direction because we overemphasize usage without thought for the overall curricular message.

If this is the case, then it becomes increasingly clear that fundamental adjustments are needed, and that we need to shift our current thoughts and sensibilities about mass education. This shift may involve deconstructing the educational setting that no longer relies on archaic practices and assumptions. What if the very foundations of mass education that were instituted during the industrial revolution are no longer appropriate for today's postmodern, sociopolitical dialogue?

With very little reflection, one would probably agree that other areas of society have undergone much sociopolitical re-shifting of the relevant model. This re-shifting is evident in areas as diverse as technology, feminism, civil rights, immigration, and the media. Whether this re-shifting is fully progressive for our society is yet to be seen, but nevertheless, it helps to bring into focus society's current state, which is transformation through change.

This raises an interesting question, however. If the system of mass education has managed to mutate to the point where it requires complexity theory to produce an analytical framework (which also implies there is no longer a central focus to guide the educational process), then is the current **educational dialectic** still appropriate for today's sociopolitical climate? Is Fullan's notion subserviently playing into education's current game of catch-up to society? Is he postulating the fact that mass education should maintain solely a reactive stance to society? And if this is the case, then to what degree are educators serving a function that promotes proactive learning? Perhaps to question at a deeper level, what precisely is the role of mass education with regards to social development?

For many, mass education is there to serve the public domain, and this should always be the case. But in order to do that more appropriately for today's society, perhaps now is the time to rethink the whole system paradigm so that it makes more sense within the larger social dialectic of the society for which mass education was meant to serve in the first place. In turn, it may be necessary to shake off the cloak of curricular tradition and engage the clientele in a more innovative curricular paradigm—one that allows for total engagement in the social dialectic currently inhabiting today's sociopolitical environment.

Currently, one may be hard-pressed to find any research that places the tome of mass education on its ear. Granted, we can still acknowledge the validity of past educational research and discussion, and it has indeed pushed the "science" of education further and further afield. But to what can we compare our current educational dialectic, if the latter is still a valid instrument for today's sociopolitical environment? It seems that the overwhelming majority of research assumes that the current *systemic identifiers* for public education will provide the best public educational blueprint. We can readily observe some of the following conventional identifiers:

- Setting up schools and colleges in buildings that resemble industrial-age factories
- Transferring preferred knowledge bases by strategically dissecting the chosen study field into specified subject areas
- Using reporting procedures that are reminiscent of modernist managerial styles
- Implementing historical reference-type curricula that are introduced primarily for analysis, evaluation, and regurgitation of "fact," and that usually have very little relevance to the current sociopolitical *dynamic* of the world
- Establishing relationships and expectations between the different parties found within the educational environment (see Zsebik 2003)

There may be other aspects that are integral to the system, but their absence in this list above does not displace the notion that the education environment is self-contained.

But is it so self-contained that it has lost its connection to the outside world?

To summarize, therefore, the main questions at stake are the following:

1. Is the current system of public education able to efficiently maintain its relevance to our society?

2. If not, then what are the challenges facing public education in relation to our postmodern society?

If we begin a dialogue with these two questions, then we can safely assume that mass education is now ready to embark on a more appropriate direction for addressing the educational needs of twenty-first-century society.

DISCUSSION AND REVIEW QUESTIONS FOR CHAPTER 2

1. Fullan claims that systems of education should be guided and not managed. If this notion was implemented, how would it impact education?

2. Discuss the notion of complexity theory and its ability to deconstruct a sociopolitical setting. Is there merit to the use of complexity theory when deconstructing an educational environment? Why or why not?

3. What is the current sociopolitical paradigm, and how is it impacting our current public education paradigm?

4. Outline current systemic identifiers for public education. How are these useful for the individual when contemplating the role of public education?

5. Explore answers to the chapter's summarizing questions that precede this review. Do they correspond to your own views on public education? Why or why not?

Chapter 3

Social and Cultural Requirements for Public Education

In the beginning, public education had a relatively simplistic function, and that was the education of the masses to fulfill the needs of that society (Zsebik 2003). Those needs ranged from inculcating the necessary rudiments for manual labor to the proper education and socialization of the elite. As society evolved from the industrial age, however, and as parents and other interested parties began to influence that educational paradigm, they placed pressure on public education so that it would evolve and remain pertinent in the face of sweeping social change.

Freire (1990) argued that the western education paradigm was politically based, and used what he termed "banking education," which will be discussed later on. Suffice to say at this point that western education is an accommodating intellectual education paradigm. What this means is that politically, the knowledge and skills taught to children are only sufficient to have them understand and function in their society, but not to change it (Zsebik 2003). Of course, social values differ within specific programs throughout the world, but again, these programs probably do not represent the vast majority of established curricula where the final outcome is an accommodating intellectual.

The educational paradigm of the twenty-first century, however, may have to focus first on the creation of a new mindset—an educational environment that's conducive to developing a ***transformative intellectual*** (ibid. 2003). This term refers to individuals who have the necessary skills and strategies to effect positive change within their sociopolitical environment. In this context, mass education must do more than "bank" or teach to the intellectual, cultural, or social norm established by the status quo. The latter is too limiting, and as suggested above, may also be counterproductive. Instead, we must create an educational paradigm that allows for a transformative learning environment. What should this paradigm look like?

To begin with, it may be appropriate to review an analysis of our current sociopolitical paradigm. As mentioned, society has become even more complex through the now-recognized development of postmodernism (since the late 1960s) and its ambivalent influence on mass education (Slattery 1995). Among others, Appadurai (Featherstone 1983) gave voice to this "complexity." Featherstone, in his book *Global Culture: Nationalism, Globalization and Modernity* provides an opportunity for Appadurai to describe society as being influenced by five cultural flows; these cultural flows determine the directions and decisions of society (please see Chapter 6 for a more detailed description).

To better visualize this different educational mindset, it may be interesting to turn to other discipline areas to see if there are models of relevance for the educational environment. In their relatively recent publication *Culture Matters,* Harrison and Huntington (2000) ponder why certain cultures are more productive economically than others:

> There have been numerous alternative theories of prosperity in this century, ranging from central planning to import substitution to factor accumulation. These ideas have become deeply rooted in societies via the educational system, the influence of intellectuals and government leaders, and countless other means... Second, economic culture appears to be heavily derived from the past and present microeconomic context... Third, social policy choices can have a strong influence on economic culture because they influence the economic context (Harrison and Huntington 2000).

These ideas are themselves cause for speculation as to how education fits within the current social paradigm, but let us just for a minute manipulate the above quote so that its focus is exclusively on education rather than economics:

> There have been numerous alternative theories of education in this century, ranging from elitist curricula to banking education curricula to accommodating curricula. These ideas have become deeply rooted in societies via the educational system itself, the influence of intellectuals and government leaders, and countless other means…Second, educational culture appears to be heavily derived from the past and present microeconomic context…Third, social policy choices can have a strong influence on educational culture because they influence the educational context.

This exercise demonstrates how both education and economics rely on the manipulation of information, on theories that attempt to promote development, and on the desire to create a more concrete, data-driven foundation to justify and promote that particular paradigm's desired results. We can also see with very little substitution that both of these social forces display extraordinary parallels. But do these areas of social influence garner the same attention? The answer to this question may cause considerable dismay.

Further, Harrison and Huntington argue that there is a constant need to revisit a paradigm structure. "There are segments of each society that hold different beliefs about what prosperity is and how it is created. Acknowledging and understanding this is the basis for creating change" (Harrison and Huntington 2000), They then show that all cultural values and beliefs do matter in the process of human progress because they shape the way individuals think about progress. They suggest the use of mental models (ibid.) to help further develop cultural knowledge bases as evidenced in the quote below:

- A mental model consists of beliefs, inferences, and goals that are first-person, concrete, and specific. It is a mental map of how the world works.

- There are sets of beliefs and attitudes that are either pro-innovation and create the proper conditions for prosperity, or anti-innovation…
- A mental model can be defined, informed, and tested around a specific, well-defined objective….
- Finally, mental models can be changed. Although culture involves the transmission of meaning from one generation to another it is unlikely that it is a genetic process (Harrison and Huntington 2000).

What these mental models say for education is huge. Perhaps they could be used as a starting point to create a more appropriate dialectic within education. Mental models could provide reference for new educational materials and objectives that would assume a multicultural education whose objective is a cultural transfiguration. This cultural transfiguration would focus on a multifaceted approach that's pertinent to today's sociopolitical environment. In other words, mass education would attempt to address the "big" questions that relate to a more thorough understanding of one's relationship to the other. It would also include addressing the challenges of rapidly changing demographic patterns, and the alienation of certain populations that may accompany these pattern changes. In every case, this paradigm would have as its focus a proactive and pro-innovative leadership role for the society it is serving.

Joseph Stiglitz, former chief economist for the World Bank, writes "that development represents a transformation of society, a movement from traditional relations, traditional ways of thinking, traditional ways of dealing with health and education, traditional methods of production(s), to modern ways" (Harrison & Huntington 2000). This begs the question that if others not in the educational environment can see the necessity for change from current practices, then should we not also be looking beyond our paradigmatic borders to determine if our traditional educational practices are appropriate for preparing the student for this rapidly developing sociopolitical environment? If not, then what is the reason that we still hold tenaciously to the systemic paradigm introduced to us in an age long past?

The question has now been posed, and the world awaits our answer which, with all humility, may be found in these next pages.

DISCUSSION AND REVIEW QUESTIONS FOR CHAPTER 3

1. Discuss the reasons for public education and how it has changed over the years. List the benefactors of these changes.

2. Explore the possibilities for public education in the future.

3. Explore how other academic disciplines may be useful to help inform our own educational decision-making processes for future directions. Why would they useful?

4. How would the use of a mental model aid in developing cultural knowledge bases? Explain why this is important for education.

CHAPTER 4

THE STORY OF EDUCATION

Ever since the first individual decided it was necessary to show something important to another individual, there has been an educational premise. Obviously, things have progressed somewhat, and what really is of import to us in this discussion begins with the notion of an organized educational system serving more than purely a "show and tell" scenario. Mass education, as it is known to the world, requires a number of elements considered essential to developing and maintaining its nature. Without these essential elements, which have incidentally been tried and tested over time, one would be hard-pressed to visualize public education in any other way.

It is interesting to note that this system of public education (which we are about to examine) can be considered self-serving. This can be seen by the simple fact that the majority of mass education concepts are internally referenced—a notion that will also be discussed later in the book. Here then is a brief overview of public education.

To begin this undertaking, it is important to establish a number of shared understandings. Indeed, there are a number of elements that comprise any academic institution, and in public education, many of these elements are universal. Using the analytical techniques outlined by Barthes in his book *Mythologies* (Barthes 1972), we hope to fully grasp the impact of different influences that affect schools and the communities that inhabit and surround those schools. In effect, the social patterns sustained in an education system, as we shall see, are a direct result of these elements.

ANALYZING POTENTIAL SIGNIFIERS FOR EDUCATION

DEFINING A SCHOOL

It is difficult to begin defining the concept of a school in general terms. The various elements that are involved within a social structure such as a school are as diverse as the individuals who inhabit this structure.

There have been numerous attempts within the educational world to create a clearer definition of a school. Beare and Slaughter, in their own research of the future of education entitled *Education for the Twenty-first Century* (1993) define the school of today as a product of the industrialization of society:

> Mass schooling, including compulsory elementary and secondary education, was a direct outcome of the industrial system." One finds within this system an abundance of factory imagery, ranging from the bureaucracy and its related positional status to graded promotion, educational terminology, the general setup of the school day, and the building in which the educational process was to occur. In fact, the big school was designed and organized like a factory (Beare and Slaughter 1993).

One need not look further than one's own neighborhood school or local newspaper to see that these agendas are still very much a part of current educational thought. Indeed, thoughts such as these do give one a better vantage from which to gauge the idea of "school" within today's society.

Imagine, however, if you were an individual who was homeschooled, perhaps due to some external factor such as geographical isolation, and had no prior experience of a school as an institution per se to draw on. Indeed, it is more than likely that the concept that individuals have concerning a school would be limited to their own experience, and it is this experiential relationship between the individual and that particular school experience that biases the conceptualization of the school. This in turn does not allow for the concept to become a universal. As found in the book *Structuralism and Education* (Gibson 1984), it also means that the conceptualization of the specified object (in this case, school as an institution) becomes both culturally and historically specific in orientation (see Chapter 9 for further discussion).

We now realize that our concept of school appears to be dependent on many culturally sensitive assumptions that affect our understanding of what makes a social entity a school, whereas personal, culturally sensitive experiences affect our understanding of the instruction that occurs within a school. In other words, individuals understand school not as the dictionary defines it, but as it applies to their own culture, which is further defined by their experiences and interpretations of that social environment.

In this particular instance, a definition of "culture" that echoes the ideas of Levi-Strauss and his premises of binary opposition and transformation (see Chapter 9) has been defined through Schein's book *Organizational Culture and Leadership* (Schein 1992):

> (Culture is) a pattern of shared basic assumptions that the group learned as it solved its problems of external adaption and internal integration, that has worked well enough to be considered valid and therefore, is to be taught to new members as the correct way to perceive, think, and feel in relation to those problems.

In other words, Schein believes that culture is created on assumptions that are shared throughout the larger community. When applied to education, we see that these assumptions inform those in the community how to function within that community. This means that one of the jobs of an educator is to ensure that students understand the social obligations of the society in which they live.

In her work on schools within the Singapore national system, Neville (1995) recognizes the importance of culture in attempting to define a school. Utilizing the above definition of culture as her basis, she defines two schools she analyzed within her study from a metaphorical aspect. The first school she described in the following way:

> The school is a plant nurtured by the teachers until it is full grown and blooms to flower ... the Principal is the gardener who prepares the ground, and gives value-added fertilizer to improve the program.

The second school she described as:

> The school is a vegetable garden with unfertile soil and seeds that are not good but due to the hard work of the Principal the school is now able to produce quality products so that he now gets better seed (ibid.).

It is interesting to note that the dominant descriptors in the second school are of "hard work," "produce," or "quality products," which imply taking raw material and making something out of it; these concepts echo Beare and Slaughter's definition of the school as an extension of the Industrial Revolution. Calvert expresses similar analogies; she devotes a chapter entitled "The Factory and the Garden" to society's metaphorical perspective on the school (Calvert 1975).

Another aspect which may prove insightful with regards to defining a school is Matthews' concept of the ethos of the international school (1989)—an educational system that relies heavily on North America's established public education concepts. In his paper, Matthews depends on Grant (1985) to define the word ethos as the following: "The Greek root of *ethos* means the habits of animals in a place ... (it) is what people in a community share that makes them a community."

This concept of the community and the ethos which it generates is of particular interest for our undertaking here, but it is unfortunately not thoroughly analyzed within Matthews's paper. Matthews's attempt to deconstruct the various factors which he considered the driving force of this ethos goes only so far as to clarify the elements of his focus on an individual basis. While this undertaking has explained several features of international schools, it does not clearly define what constitutes an "international education," and ipso facto, an international school. By the same token, and despite the remarkable similarities between the international and public systems (see Zsebik 2003), Matthews's theories also fail to substantiate the environmental ethos for public education as well. It also provides little (if any) guidance as to how this ethos may be defined or measured in this school environment. However, it is arguably this "interactive ethos" of the school community that can provide a preliminary guide for defining the essence of a school. It doesn't matter where the school is situated—the ethos relies on the interconnectedness of elements that are within the school community. Combined with the culture surrounding the school, these elements create and define the institutional character of the school.

In order to further understand the elements of a school environment, we should be aware of yet another deconstruction process of those elements. The latter are readily apparent and can be summarized as follows:

S tudent
P arent
A dministration   =   The SPACE Factor
C urriculum
E ducator

We will be discussing the SPACE Factor shortly, but first let's go over the analysis process that has been utilized to frame the coming discussion.

DEFINING THE CONCEPT OF SCHOOL AND ITS COMMUNITY

Barthes, whose philosophical leanings tended to change over his lifetime, was nevertheless instrumental in bringing the notion of semiological analysis to public attention. In his preface, Barthes writes:

> I had just read Saussure and as a result acquired a conviction that by treating "collective representations" as sign-systems, one might hope to go further than the pious show of unmasking them and account in detail for the mystification which transforms petit-bourgeois culture into a universal nature (Barthes 1974).

Although Barthes' writing is sometimes complex in nature, it does manage to explain his thinking process and our application to education. While Barthes' main focus at this point was to open the eyes of the general public to what he considered their inability to distinguish between fiction and reality in everyday situations, his work still provides some insight into the nature of an academic institution. In the above quotation, if we were to replace "collective representations" with "school and those elements outlined by SPACE," and if we replaced "petit-bourgeois culture" with "ethos, culture, and community of the school," a working representation of the subject at hand will have evolved. The reworded quote would read like this:

> By treating the terms school and those elements outlined within the SPACE Factor semiologically, one might hope to go further than unmasking them within an empirical framework and account in detail for the mystification which (in turn) will transform the ethos, culture, and community of the school into a universal nature (Zsebik 2003).

While again the complex nature of the subject may be daunting, it does help to clarify how a school as an institution can be broken down. Therefore to continue this discussion, we will first outline the concept of semiology. Semiology can be defined as the science that deals with signs, symbols, and their impact on the society using them. According to Barthes (ibid.), when dealing with any semiological concept, we must address three terms on an equal footing. Those three terms are called the *signifier*, the *signified*, and the *sign*. At first glance, the signifier and the signified are directly related. Barthes uses the example of "a bunch of roses." In this case, the phrase "bunch of roses" is the signifier for the object in question, which is also, at the same time, the signified. This semiological system, however, contains another essential element. When the phrase "bunch of roses" enters the domain of human interaction, it implies passion or love—and this hidden communiqué is called the sign.

The interaction that Barthes developed between the word and the object, and their ability to communicate a specific concept, proves an interesting, enlightening approach when it is applied to an educational institution and its elements.

When discussing such an ambiguous concept as school, and those basic parts that were outlined above, however, one must find some solid footing from which to depart analytically.

To begin achieving this better footing, one must first turn one's attention again to the aptly-named mnemonic SPACE, which was chosen to summarize the elements found within a school.

Firstly, the physical space a school utilizes would have little relevant meaning if these elements were not to **interact** to form a community. At the same time, this community could not be created without the SPACE that the school provides: in other words, the school combines students, parents, administration, curricular programs, and educators within a physical establishment. It is within this SPACE that the community, and therefore the school and its educational agendas, are defined. In effect, an ideal representation of the interactive framework found within a specific educational setting has been established.

Secondly, SPACE refers to the elements within the **community**, not only in physical but abstract terms—see Hofstede (1991) below. It also plays a significant part in determining the outcome of the school's ethos. Within this context, communication and interaction between each element within the school SPACE becomes an essential aspect of the paradigm created within each specific institution.

Thirdly, the SPACE is **dependent** on the five separate entities that constitute its elements. But if one of these entities were replaced or removed, then the word SPACE and the concept it defines would be lost. There is an inseparable connection between these five entities, just as with their letter representations in the word, which cannot be altered without serious consequence to the concept.

To summarize: the SPACE of a school identifies a school's *interactive communal dependence* within that school environment.

THE SEMIOTICS OF THE SPACE FACTOR

The next step is to define the parameters into which the elements found within SPACE fall. While it might appear at first glance that very little academic insight is required to define these elements, there is in reality a need for a more in-depth analysis. It is important that a definitive perspective be allowed to surface to prevent assumptions from occurring, otherwise the final result would lack the clarity this process hopes to provide.

If we utilize the process which Barthes' outlined, we can begin with the Longman Dictionary (1987) to identify society's interpretation of the object *(the signified),* of the *signifier* (the word), and we can begin to define the semiotic parameters of our SPACE Factor. When determining the *sign,* however, then one must begin to ask the following questions:

- Why has this signifier come into existence?
- What sociological imperative drives the signifier's existence?
- What expectations does society place on those aspects that receive identity from their signifier?
- What relationships exist between the signifier and other related signifiers?

These questions provide a clear process from which the sign of each element in the SPACE Factor can be formulated.

If we were to draft a general answer to these questions, it might read like this:

- The signifiers with which we are dealing came into existence because there was a need to label regularly recognized characteristics within the field of education.
- The imperative which drives the signifier's existence is its usefulness to society.
- Expectations of society might be defined according to the outcome expected of the signifier in question.
- The signifiers are perhaps the most important aspect of these questions, as it provides an accurate signpost for the signifier's functions and real intentions as a sign within the academic environment.

The questions outlined above serve as useful starting points to define the elements in the SPACE Factor semiologically.

THE STUDENT

"Student" is thus defined semiologically:
Signifier: Student
Signified: A person who is studying at a place of education.
Sign: A developing human being who is learning to function effectively within a given society.

THE PARENT

Signifier: Parent
Signified: The father or mother of a person
Sign: An individual who protects, feeds, nurtures, and shelters the student outside the educational institution. (In some instances, the role of the parent is partially transferred to the school, especially in a boarding school situation.)

THE ADMINISTRATION

Signifier: Administration
Signified: The management or direction of affairs of a business, government, or school.
Sign: Individuals who maintain the organizational structure where the recipients of the service (the Student and the Parent), and the suppliers of the service (the curriculum and the educator) can interact.

It is interesting to note at this point that the 'A' in Administration falls neatly between the four other Factors (SP and CE) within the SPACE mnemonic, serving also as a visual representation of the pivotal and political role administration plays within an educational structure—that of balancing the needs and wishes of the other elements; in this case the clients (student and parent) and the service (curriculum and educators)

THE CURRICULUM

Signifier: Curriculum
Signified: A course of study offered at school (or other place of learning)

Sign: A collective representation of society's prioritization toward the available knowledge bases; what that society deems as important knowledge to transfer to the learner or Student.

THE EDUCATOR

Signifier: Educator
Signified: A person who educates, especially as a profession.
Sign: An individual whose responsibility is to maintain the security of the student, to serve as a role model or temporary replacement (*in loco parentis*) for the parent, to meet the expectations of the administration, and to oversee the implementation of the curriculum.

From this vantage point, we can see that the educator is the foundation from which all other aspects of the educational institution build. In other words, the SPACE Factor serves as another testament to the importance of the teacher within an educational structure. The significance of this aspect, however, does not undermine the need for other elements to be present within this structure. As a matter of fact, the role of the educator would not exist if the other elements were not also available. This interactive interdependence is in effect what makes a school a school. It extends equally over every element found within the SPACE Factor and constitutes the ethos of the academic environment. As was previously mentioned, none of the elements would be able to exist without the other four being present. For instance, a boarding school would probably have a very low level of parental involvement in the school's activities, and for this reason, the ethos of that boarding school would be very different from perhaps a day school where parental involvement may be at a much higher level.

Before we apply Barthes's ideas to the signifier school, a further step is required: recycling the sign to become the new signifier. This is the process Barthes uses to address a "myth" concept. He surmises that a two-step process is essential to strip away the myth surrounding a particular social concept, leaving only the bare essentials open for further scrutiny.

Is the school a myth? In Barthes' sense of the word, it is. He stressed that everything can be surrounded by myth, and from this he believed that "Myth is not defined by the object of its message, but by the way in which it utters its message." In other words, a concept such as a school can only be rooted in its own myth, and this myth is defined by the common language and vocabulary associated with that particular environment. Therefore what we know about a school is limited to the communication and language patterns that surround it.

The phrase "school as a myth" can have a more specific translation: "school as an entity that depends on its communicative nature for its existence." This aspect will be further analyzed later, but for now, suffice it to say that the *concept* of *a school in a society is a myth rooted in general speculation and superficial observances because of its reliance on human interpretation within that society as the source of its existence.* In other words, there is no means to establish a concrete definition without potentially alienating the concept to reality. Therefore, a school remains a "mythical" concept rooted in the assumptions generated by interrelationships. The latter are created between the individuals of the environment and the perceptions and interactivity of the individuals in that environment. We can also add that school as an environment is defined by the daily operations of the academic environment.

To proceed, we find Barthes' two-step analysis will predictably lead to a more in-depth perspective concerning the original signifier, in this case, the school. Barthes (1974) used the following diagram to illustrate this process:

1.Signifier   2.Signified

3.SIGN

i. Signifier   *ii. Signified*

iii. SIGN

Fig. 4.1 – *Two-step deconstruction process as outlined by Barthes to define a "mythical" concept within a society.*

Utilizing this schematic, we come to the following conceptualization, taking note of the font format to represent the different levels and their overlapping significances:

1. Signifier   School

2. Signified   A place to gather for learning purposes

3. SIGN & *I. Signifier*   A communal collection of ideas and individuals that dynamically interacts within the physical structure that determines the educational outcome of the learner

       ii. Signified   The SPACE Factor

       iii. SIGN   Proliferation of the socio - political paradigm that the SPACE Factor has or wishes to establish

Fig 4.2 – *Deconstruction of School using Barthes's Theory of Analysis*

This analysis demonstrates that the ethos of a school is a sociopolitical creation made through the SPACE factor, which in turn creates the paradigm of a school. This paradigm then defines and sets the priorities for the school.

By the same token, the school defines the SPACE Factor, thereby also establishing the social paradigm that in turn defines the ethos. We can thus treat the paradigm in an educational environment as a variable that will change the entire definition process.

DISCUSSION AND REVIEW QUESTIONS FOR CHAPTER 4

1. Based on your own experiences as an educator, how would you define a school? Are your experiences comparable to those stated in the chapter? Draw a table listing your experiences and those concepts found in the chapter for a comparative analysis.

2. Below on the same piece of paper, draw a Venn diagram to outline the similarities and differences between your experiences and those outlined in this chapter.

3. What assumptions are necessary to understand the premise of a school?

4. Discuss how the following notions help to deconstruct the notion of school
   a) Culture
   b) Ethos
   c) SPACE Factor

5. Outline Barthes' philosophical theory of deconstruction. How does it help understand the school environment?

6. Outline the reasons why SPACE can serve as a suitable mnemonic to summarize the elements of a school environment.

CHAPTER 5

SHARED SOCIAL AND POLITICAL RELATIONSHIPS IN A SCHOOL

Generally speaking, shared social and political relationships primarily refer to the undercurrents that interact in an institution. In his comments on the relationship between church and state (CNN World Report, October 4, 1997), Jim Clancy stated that whenever a number of like-minded people come together to form a community, political features arise. Inevitably, there are individuals within that community who want to spread their ideas and influences; they believe that their perception of reality is the best. Unfortunately, this perception may not be appropriate for those affected, whether this ideological tendency influences them directly or indirectly.

From a political standpoint, these different perceptions of reality may be neatly divided along a spectrum. The following diagram summarizes those perceptions:

----------------/------------------/--------------------/------------------------/-------------------

Radical   **Liberal**   **Moderate**   **Conservative** **Reactionary**

Fig. 5.1 *Diagram of the Political Spectrum*

Since the school consists of a community of individuals who have come together for a specific purpose, then this creates a political situation (see Chapter 10). This is due primarily to the school's established task of indoctrinating young people into the norms and ideas of the society to which the institution belongs. The school as a community has a political mandate that must fall somewhere along the spectrum shown above.

The question is: how can one determine a school's placement along this spectrum? To determine this, it may be helpful to look at the "product" of the school—in other words, the student. To be more precise, the type of individual the school produces will allow us to distinguish a school's sociopolitical structure or paradigm.

Freire (1990) coherently summarized the different types of intellectual outcomes that a learner can achieve. Using the same type of diagram, these can be summarized as follows:

Transformative intellect Critical intellect Accommodating intellect Hegemonic intellect
----------------------------/-----------———-------/--------------------------------/------------------------

Fig. 5.2 *Diagram of Freire's Intellectual Outcomes*

- *Transformative* intellectuals are individuals who have the opportunity to utilize their intellectual powers to solve problems. They deal critically with issues that bear relevance to immediate or future educational and social situations, and work to effect transformations
- *Critical* intellectuals are those who have received the necessary skills and information to identify the problems and opportunities in their environment. However, their criticism falls short of action. They lack the impetus or intellectual scope to affect serious change.
- *Accommodating* intellectuals are aware of the needs, problems, and opportunities of their environment, but they attempt very little to affect change due to their belief that nothing will change.
- *Hegemonic* intellectuals are those who have only adopted limited relationships with the dominant group due primarily to a limited access to information that helps to maintain the status quo of the dominant group.

The end results, when the two diagrams are superimposed, appear as follows:

Transformative Intellect	Critical intellect	Accommodating intellect	Hegemonic intellect

```
-------------------/------------------------/-------------------/------------------------
```

Radical	Liberal	Moderate	Conservative	Reactionary

Fig. 5.3 *Diagram of Intellectual Outcomes and Their Political Affiliations*

We can justify superimposing the intellectual outcome of an individual's education and its political affiliations if we observe cause and effect. A transformative intellectual will react to situations with the notion of change in mind where the **hegemonic** intellectual will react with the notion of keeping things as they are. In effect it now becomes much clearer how the education system can and does shape the intellectual capabilities of individual learners, and how this focus can be observed on the political spectrum. Political motivation has been defined where left wing liberal (radical) tendencies are focused to affect change and where right wing conservative (reactionary) tendencies are focused on the maintenance of current situations. While this may be an oversimplification of the political spectrum, it does provide a guide for analysis of a situation we have construed as political.

Hicks and Holden (1995) also press for more political definition, which is very similar to that developed above. They have divided their ideological orientations in the following manner:

Conservative
School prepares students for work and it maintains and legitimizes existing social, economic, and political structures. The framework includes formal classrooms to teach subjects, to transmit knowledge through directive transmission. Within a conservative ideology, a school's purpose is to help students learn their place in society.

Reformative
School prepares students to participate in the reform of society. Classrooms are more informal and

individualized, and there is a less rigid framework to teach subjects. Within a reformative ideology, a school facilitates learning through a "person-centered approach." Its purpose is to help students learn who they are.

Transformative
School and society reflect one another. Group work considers students' mixed abilities. There are flexible boundaries between the school and community, and the teacher is viewed as a resource person. Within a transformative ideology, the school plays a role in challenging social, political, and economic inequalities. Its purpose is to educate students who will transform themselves and society.

Guiding a school's political orientation presents added difficulty, however. It requires defining the appropriate paradigm a school must formulate. This is an important step that educators must take, not necessarily to change the curriculum, but rather to change *how* the curriculum is addressed. This means that there is a need to identify the sociopolitical agenda of the school community. Once we accomplish this overview, it will become easier to see where we are and to establish if there is a need to redefine the educational environment, based on whether or not the resulting political orientation adequately meets the needs of that community.

It is this author's opinion that public education for the twenty-first century should have an international perspective that focuses on social responsibility, achieved through a critical thinking orientation. At this point, it would be easy to enter into a lengthy discussion of the merits of a more localized or isolated educational orientation over those of an international orientation. However, such an isolated education system ignores the bigger picture of our society.

In contrast, our new narrative would include providing access to all knowledge and cultures through both the available technology and the surrounding society. In other words, education must embrace society as an integral part of the classroom learning so that this new narrative would be able to aid all students who live in this ever-more complex environment.

From here it also becomes easier to see the merits of using the SPACE Factor as a starting point for framing a school's academic purpose. Defining these different elements in your school community allows us to see the potential challenges and possibilities of creating an appropriate twenty-first century educational environment.

DISCUSSION AND REVIEW QUESTIONS FOR CHAPTER 5

1. In the political spectrum explored in this chapter, discuss where you would currently place your own institution. Why?

2. Explore and discuss the reasons why your institution is currently on this particular part of the spectrum.

3. On which portion of the spectrum would you like to position your institution? Why? Is this position different from where you currently stand? Why?

4. List the opportunities in your academic environment that could help redefine your institution.

Chapter 6

Historical and Contemporary Insights

The idea of educating has been an integral part of any organized society throughout the history of mankind. In early times, leaders who devoted their lives to the development of their society recognized the need to educate the populace, in the hope that this education would guarantee a better chance of survival. We are not absolutely certain about the curriculum and methodologies that were used in the distant past, however, it is safe to speculate that prior to the advent of modernism, education primarily took the form of master-apprentice relationships and shared knowledge, where learned individuals provided education to both rulers and followers. Those who took on the role of the teacher were invariably people of experience, and they may have come from different areas of society, including perhaps family members, individuals in the community, medicine men, elders, and religious figures.

Gammage (1971) echoes these ideas:

> ...often in primitive communities, mothers and other women teach the children what and how to eat and speak. Fathers and other men teach the children how to hunt, fish or grow crops (though here the sex differences must be borne in mind); and the medicine men or witch-

doctors initiate the young into much of the tribal lore and culture.

Including education into the social fabric is still prevalent today. The educational experience with which we are currently familiar utilizes Oriental, Greek, and Middle Eastern philosophies and the dominant organized religions of the world (e.g. Christianity, Buddhism, Islam, and Judaism). These sources, coupled with the academic influences of the "so-called intermediate societies of India, Greece, Rome, etc.," (Gammage 1971), helped to provide educational guidance.

We can also see the responsibilities that education has taken on during the course of its relational development with society. Regardless of whether education is acquired by apprenticeship or through university seminars, or, as Spring (1998) suggested, as a means "to bring 'civility' to the uncivilized in the New World...," what is noteworthy is that education must focus on a specific purpose within its context, and this is accomplished through the chosen curricular structure. In other words, the way the curriculum is structured can achieve specific educational purposes within the context of the society it aims to serve.

Conversely, an education that bears no relationship to the society in which it is found becomes an isolated and perhaps useless activity. It is this author's belief, therefore, that the act of acquiring an education must hold relevance for the individual taking part in the process. This implies that the spectrum of instruction should range from the pure acquisition of facts and skills, to the grounding and development of one's creative forces, or to achieving philosophical insights.

This, therefore, implies that education should address all knowledge bases without exception. Regardless of a society's sociopolitical orientation, every area of knowledge that prepares learners to live within their society must be given equal credibility. Durkheim for instance suggested, during the modernist era, that mass education was to foster social solidarity and national cohesion (Durkheim 1977), while Green states later on that the role of mass education appears to promote a national popular cultural hegemony (consistency) that's defined mainly by the dominant classes (Green 1997).

We see in retrospect that the demands western society placed on education were relatively clear. Change in past educational practices may have occurred through an evolutionary process, or it may have taken form due to conquest or diplomacy. During the Middle Ages, and up until the Renaissance, organized western religion played a two-sided educational game. On the one hand, it educated selected individuals, but on the other, it also served as a social check against radical change in thought. During the Renaissance, however, as the age of enlightenment began to take hold of western civilization, several developments in western civilization began to erode this static situation.

Following the conquests of the Ottoman Empire in the fifteenth century, change really began to take hold. Refugees began to flood into Italy, bringing with them their own cultural "baggage," which affected "the political, religious and economic domains..." (Lang 1963) of the countries that accepted them. In the sixteenth century, along with this reawakening of the collective mind, the nation-state of Italy was created. This social development attempted to incorporate two modes of thinking:

> They retained the idea of universalism, but theirs was a nonpolitical empire of fantasy, virtue, art, and learning... Oddly enough, politically they were anti-universal, championing the newly born idea of nationalism (Lang 1963).

This new social mindset characterized much of what occurred during the Enlightenment era, which was an ongoing development of the ideas inspired by this "rebirth." Within this context came the desire of others to develop a different and more utopian society. Thinkers like Thomas Jefferson, Benjamin Franklin, and Karl Marx echoed these concepts, giving rise to the political concepts of democracy, socialism, and communism in their various forms, which to this day shape the majority of the political and educational agendas of the world. The time period when nationalism was high on the political agenda in the West also proved to be a strong influence on developing educational institutions in those countries undergoing such changes.

On the historical heels of this change in political current came another factor that significantly influenced today's current social situation—the Industrial Revolution. This industrialization process not only had far-reaching effects on production technique and business, it also determined a new course for education. Beare and Slaughter

(1993) argue that the industrial revolution played a significant role in transforming the practice of education from its master-apprentice stance to that of the large bureaucratic model.

As Weber put it (in Beare and Slaughter), large-scale organization at this point in history was considered the "ideal form" a business could take for success:

> It was predictable, its purpose and operations were rational, its routines were systematic and rarely changed, and it was large-scale, capable of making routine the activities of literally thousands of people. It was an organizational structure built on the analogy to a machine (Beare and Slaughter 1993).

Beare and Slaughter continue that "since mass schooling, including compulsory elementary and secondary education, was a direct outcome of the industrial system," one finds within a school an abundance of factory imagery, ranging from the bureaucracy and its related positional status to graded promotion, educational terms and labels, the general setup of the school day, and the building in which the educational process was to occur. "In fact, the big school was designed and organized like a factory" (ibid.), and one need not look further than one's neighborhood school to see that these same organizational systems are still today very much a part of educational thought. If we add to this Green's concept of cultural consistency (Green 1997) (as stated above), we begin to see a clearer picture of the demands placed on education. Interestingly, Green furthers his argument that countries have differing educational policies because of state formation rather than industrialization, urban development, or social control (ibid. 1997). Regardless, however, the model for education appears to have its roots in business organization.

Bowles and Gintis (1976) also believe in this idea that the construction of the education environment is due to the social relationships found in education: the relationships between administrators and teachers, teachers and students, students and students, and students and their work. These social relationships mirror traditional relationships in the workplace, and are reflected in students' lack of control over their own education, the alienation of the student from the curriculum content, and the use of a system of grades and other external rewards to motivate students to finish their work.

Armitage (1974) summarizes that the forces of change during this period of western history gradually brought about a number of wide-ranging and acute policy-setting agendas for education in the west. A description of some of these historical changes can be summarized through:

- the creation of a custodial imperative
- the creation of an ideology
- the question of internal dynamics
- the creation of a startle pattern

Armitage explains the terms very eloquently for the time he is describing, and so an extended quotation would produce a more vivid description of these principles (ibid.):

The Custodial Imperative
If you exclude children from factories by act of parliament, or technological improvements take place, you have to put them somewhere, so you put them in school. Thus the custodial imperative becomes the impetus to educational legislation ... Once children were in schools, it was discovered that all sorts of things were wrong with them (the children) ... (They were) underfed ... unwanted ... (and) so what is called the protective perimeter ... garrisoned by the armies of social workers and counselors ... had to be thrown up.

The Ideology
Secondly, such containment of children demands an ideology if not a theology. One cannot force children into a school and say "we will teach them how to enjoy their leisure." No society has yet discovered how to enjoy leisure ... You have to work and you have to work at something. This something is called the curriculum. The curriculum is what is good for you, not what you want.

The Question of Internal Dynamics

The third principle ... is the question of internal dynamics. Once young people are contained too long in school or college, and their status as adults is deferred, one cannot say, as The Observer did: "There will be no revolution: Official!" Another internal dynamic comes from the staff who want to improve the condition not only of their charges, but of themselves as well. So the long upward haul of the teacher's profession begins ...

The Startle Pattern

This means the influence of one country on another ... "Startle" means that one country gets very frightened by another ...

The "Startle Pattern" Armitage refers to is competitiveness and the fear of missing out. If one country is utilizing advanced materials and methodology in the classroom, this may help its students gain an educational advantage that would, in turn, gain an economic edge for the nation. When this happens, other countries may fear missing out on that advantage.

It is worth noting that of the four principles that Armitage describes, three are rooted in the curricular structure a school may adopt. "The Question of Internal Dynamics" (ibid.), for instance, is constantly being defined by the demands of the education environment and the curriculum it promotes. All relationships between staff and students, between the staff and administrators, and even between staff and parents are somehow modified by the school's educational structure. By the same token, we can argue that there are influential elements in the school environment that affect the educational structure, resulting in a dialogue about the most suitable education environment for that situation.

With regard to the Startle Pattern, however, the question arises as to whether this notion is still fully relevant in today's social environment. Businesses of today appear to be unconcerned about national boundaries for their marketplace, and even federal governments see that cooperation between countries is the better solution in today's economic climate. This author would argue, however, that the "Startle Pattern" of today has followed the postmodernist route and is not just between *nations.* Instead, it has extended to the level of the individual as can evidenced by pressure from parents on the school to ensure the best available educational environment for their child.

The "Creation of an Ideology" is also closely tied to the Startle Pattern, which is problematic. The current problem of change in today's society makes it extraordinarily difficult to achieve a suitable and current focus for public education. If a curriculum is to exhibit contemporary meaning, however, then this implies that the curriculum (at all levels as defined in Chapter 1) must be grounded in fundamental concepts that consistently address the needs of the society it is meant to serve. This also suggests the need to analyze the current social environment for the most effective educational focus.

But the question which now arises is whether these agendas are still justifiable in today's "global village," postmodern society, or whether they are mementos of an educational structure created for a nationalist, focused, industrial society of the past.

Today, the ideological principles of national school systems that Armitage outlined are being challenged primarily by more financial, regional, and "international" objectives that will inevitably affect the educational landscape. One outstanding example affecting education is the fading reliance on geopolitical boundaries to control trade; these are being replaced by treaty alliances such as the GATT Treaty, the NAFTA Agreement, and the European Union.

> The treaty process can be considered a major factor in the development of a common civic culture across geographical distances and social differences ... Treaties can be either bilateral or multilateral ... (but) because of the unpopularity of the concept of multilateralism among the major powers, the problem of coordinating behaviours of sovereign nation-states in situations where cooperation is essential has led to the adoption of the concept of regime (Keohane & Nye 1985; see also Johansen 1986) as an alternative to multilateralism. International regimes are rules and procedures that define the limits of acceptable behaviour on various issues ... (and) because the concept of regime minimizes

structure and gives the emphasis to interests and values, it provides a promising new instrument for civic culture in new arenas where it does not now exist" (Boulding 1988).

From this perspective, we can argue that a move away from nationalism, which has dominated Western political thinking, has shifted to a thinking pattern of globalization (Green1997). In effect, the agreements mentioned above appear to reflect a certain awareness that things are changing, and a struggle has ensued over how to best maintain the interests that various national systems have acquired.

It is now apparent that changes in society have a direct influence on that society's educational environment. These changes may not have been implemented until some other motivating factor proved their necessity, such as the rebuilding of Europe after World War II through the Marshall Plan (Spring 1998), but they still tend to reflect what is occurring in that society at the time. Based on this argument, and judging by the state of today's "global" society, now may be the time to reconsider education's current position in the sociopolitical environment, and therefore whether education should once more think to redefine its curricular goals. At this point, however, it is necessary to focus on a more contemporary overview of education to determine if this supposition has any grounding.

A CONTEMPORARY OVERVIEW OF EDUCATION

Educators make daily decisions about what knowledge and skills are relevant to teach. The aim of these decisions is to determine the direction that educators must take in the classroom to cater to their students' needs.

Once the educator, the institution, and the system decide upon those things that they consider important, there is still the danger these priorities may be out of sync with the society the system hopes to serve. This danger can come from anywhere, and it could include issues that arise from within the system itself (see Chapter 4) to external forces that suddenly place pressure on the educational environment. The end result could be a somewhat vicious circle as educators try to identify the needs of society, but once they've decided on the policies to implement, change inevitably occurs and their decisions once more become irrelevant to the needs of the learner within the current climate. This cycle is demonstrated clockwise below:

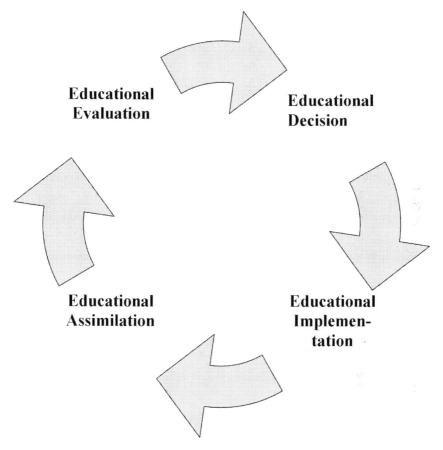

Fig. 6.1 *The current educational decision-making cycle*

This cycle that has been outlined could serve as a brief summary of the situation that many educational environments face today. Around the world, politicians are seemingly quick to point a finger at education for not preparing their people well enough for today's society. Indeed, the news media and other sources (e.g., TIMSS data, OECD studies, etc.) readily publish educational reports that statistically announce where each country stands on the educational standard scale; these reports usually add to the general feeling of education's inadequacies. Whether one is able to argue with what is printed is another question, but the media's tendency to focus on the ills of society, and its willingness to embrace education as being a part of that category may prove more than just a distortion of reality. The slightest objection, whether or not it's truthful, should in every case spur educators to critically examine current educational practice.

To be fair, current education systems are not fully to blame; the state of society and the developments it embraces are progressing at an exceptional rate, and the bureaucratic system in which these educational systems are embedded may not have the flexibility to do anything more than some political tinkering. This mindset can make it extraordinarily difficult for education to keep up with the current pace of development. But then shouldn't there be some effort to solve the problem? Perhaps the reason for this is that society itself is having difficulty pinpointing its needs because of constant change. If this is the case, then education may also have difficulty focusing.

One solution may be to search for features within the human experience to provide a more fitting educational framework.

The present problem may not only be an inability to identify and deal with recent changes in society, but it may also tie into society's potential future directions. Appadurai has attempted to outline the reasons for present and future developments within society as "Global Cultural flows" (Featherstone 1993), or those dynamic and influential forces shaping the social climate of our contemporary world. Appadurai suggests that:

> There are five dimensions of Global Cultural flows that move in non-isomorphic paths. Firstly, there are *ethnoscapes* produced by flows of people: tourists, immigrants, refugees, exiles, and guest workers. Secondly, there are *technoscapes*, the machinery and plant flows produced by multinational and national corporations and government agencies. Thirdly, there are *finanscapes*, produced by the rapid flows of money in the currency markets and stock exchanges. Fourthly, there are *mediascapes*, the repertoires of images and information, the flows which are produced and distributed by newspapers, magazines, television and

film. Fifthly, there are *ideoscapes*, linked to flows of images which are associated with state or counter-state movement ideologies which are comprised of elements of the Western Enlightenment world-view—images of democracy, freedom, welfare, rights, etc.

Appadurai's views suggest a one-way flow, from western to non-western cultures. This may indeed be the case as western countries generally hold the power and wealth necessary to induce movement within these flows. Nevertheless, there is no reason to suppose that these flows go exclusively in one direction; thanks to twenty-first-century technology, this is especially true in today's information-rich society. In addition, one must add the element of various agencies who attempt to control these dimensions (Appadurai 1993); these flows, in turn, have a direct influence on the educational environment.

When we take all of the above into account, we can begin to see the enormity of the task that educators face. Public education's effectiveness in this present age must integrate a thorough understanding of these cultural flows, so that it can best determine which information would be of most value to the learner. Somewhat tentatively, there have been attempts to address the most visible, and therefore, perhaps the most obvious of these cultural flows—the media.

As an example, in the late 1980s, the Ontario Ministry of Education in Canada introduced a series of courses for each grade level labeled "Media Literacy." In each of these graded courses, students were given the opportunity to "deconstruct" the various media, allowing them to better understand the effects and pervasiveness of the media within society. Since the program was initiated, however, the course has undergone constant revision to maintain its relevance to external social changes. This is no fault of the Ontario Ministry. Indeed, the Ministry has been on top of these changes at all levels. The point here is that the pace of technological innovation has created a challenge to public education's curricular guidelines to an extent that's been unparalleled in history. To their credit, we find that the Ministry has recently adopted the notion of incorporating Media Literacy into the standard English-classroom program. Not only that, but the Ministry also provides guidelines for a whole other program that focuses on developing the necessary skills for communications technology. The latter program includes all the resources needed to make it successful. What this says is that public education has recognized the importance of this cultural flow, but while these courses are a positive undertaking to lead the learner towards a cultural awareness of the media, in today's society it may be more appropriate to identify the mediascape in relation to the other flows suggested above. It may be that these flows, although easily identifiable and isolated as Appadurai suggests, still need to be seen within the context of the broader picture. In effect a course of this nature would be more contemporary if it were to address the interactivity of these different cultural flows in our society.

Additionally, despite educators' apparent desire to promote what they consider to be important for the learners, the reality of the situation is that what may be taught inside the classroom could bear no relevance to that which is found outside the classroom. With the media's daily bombardment to promote their own well-organized agenda, mass education and schooling as a vehicle for information dissemination may eventually find itself inadequate and obsolete.

In fact, schools and school systems are facing a new and unprecedented layer of Startle Pattern: Now it not only includes the fact that each country or individual may be comparing itself to the other (as in the Armitage scenario above), but they must also begin to think along the broader concept of globalization. This author believes the new startle pattern can be attributed to four things which are closely aligned with Appadurai's findings:

- an increase in global business patterns and its related competitiveness (*finanscapes*)
- the rapid advancement of communications technology and its contribution towards global interconnectedness (*technoscapes*)
- changing social patterns and their related social issues (*ideoscapes*)
- increased immigration of peoples to different areas of the world (*ethnoscapes*)
- competition from the media as a source of information that transcends not only the boundaries of a nation but also

that country's own specific cultural identity (*mediascapes, ethnoscapes, and ideoscapes*).

From this perspective, we can now see that educational systems must evaluate themselves differently to determine if they are not only preparing the learner to function within a national context, but if they are also providing a perspective that prepares students for a much more complex world than ever before. In brief, where once the culture of the country lent a natural bent to the curriculum, we must now question whether the material we're teaching is relevant to the demands and needs of today's social environment. (See Fig. 7.1 on page 87 for a visual representation of the different levels.)

DISCUSSION AND REVIEW QUESTIONS FOR CHAPTER 6

1. Using this chapter as your resource, draw a rough chronological timeline summarizing the role of education through the ages of man.
2. Discuss the possible reasons for any major changes that education has undergone.
3. Outline what particular social agendas led to the development of mass public education.
4. Draw a table that outlines how the different social forces (e.g., The Startle Pattern) contributed to today's education environment.
5. What new social influence appears to have intruded on contemporary educational mindsets? Why is this potentially a problem?
6. Provide examples from your own experiences that relate to the educational decision-making cycle. Provide examples that do not relate to this same cycle. Why are these examples different?
7. What are some of the issues concerning education's apparent challenges to maintaining an efficient and effective public education system?
8. Discuss Appadurai's deconstruction of society and its relationship to public education.

CHAPTER 7

THE BROADER PICTURE FOR PUBLIC EDUCATION

Several labels can be associated with education in the world. The variety of these labels may be an attempt to better describe the focus of the curriculum. If this is the case, then it is imperative to analyze these different labels in order to understand what constitutes an "international education."

NATIONS, NATIONALS, AND NATIONALISM

It is perhaps most effective to begin with what had the most impact on education and its social environment. We will therefore start with the idea of *nations*, the political concept which saw the birth of the mass education system.

Although the *Fontana Dictionary of Modern Thought* (Bullock 1988) does not list the term "national," it does list "nationalism," giving more than one account of how this term is applied in today's society:

> **Nationalism.** (1) The feeling of belonging to a group united by common racial, linguistic and historical ties, and usually identified with a particular territory. (2) A corresponding ideology which exalts the nation as

state as the ideal form of political organization with an overriding claim on the loyalty of its citizens.

The dictionary then describes the historic rise in nationalism and its variations, including Mazzini's (1805–72) interpretation of the "principle of nationality," which saw "the individual nations as subdivisions of a larger world society that should live together in peace." If only Mazzini's nineteenth-century interpretation were a reality!

Reality, however, took on more volatile forms, and these forms, as outlined in *The Fontana Dictionary* (ibid.) included:

- *Integrative* nationalism which comes in the shape of imperialism
- *Territorial* nationalism as a response toward the desire to maintain national boundaries after decolonization
- *Ethnic* nationalism as expressed in the violence of the Balkans, the U.K., Spain, Italy, as well as certain African conflicts
- *Pan or Super-State* nationalism which attempts to bring together geographically or culturally similar units of society (e.g., Pan-Islam)

From this perspective, it becomes clearer how nations may perceive themselves and their *raisons d'être*. It also implies that to promote a particular national perspective, education is often a vehicle for promoting one or more of the aspects listed above. Spring (*Education and the Rise or the Global Economy* 1998) offers a good portion of his book to demonstrate this trait, emphasizing that education is a tool of the modern state to encourage and ensure its sovereignty against other nations.

Let us proceed further with some concepts of "nation" and "nationalism" and their ties to education. Mallinson (*An Introduction to the Study of Comparative Education* 1975) in his book on comparative education sees the function of national education as "a social force and ... that of assuring cultural continuity mainly through fostering the growth and development of national characteristics that will act as a stabilizing force." Mallinson then defines culture as "those capabilities acquired by man (woman) to make of him (her) an acceptable member of the society to which he (she) belongs." At the same time, Jeffreys (ibid., 1975) defines the purpose of education at the national level as: "The nurture of personal growth" and most especially, "the conserving, transmitting, and renewal of culture."

It seems that one essential element of a national education is the creation and development of a cultural identity, which from Mallinson's viewpoint forms the basis of a national identity. It is the duty of each state to foster this national identity in anticipation of an attack from an external presence. One could visualize the function of this national identity as the white blood cells of a body, where these cells' main function is to fight off infection from an outside source—in this case a political or physical source. Each nation, therefore, may attempt to transmit distinct social characteristics through its education system. The success of these nations in their development of this so-called immune system may now lead to sociopolitical complications with other nations which may otherwise have proved beneficial in today's social environment. This is similar to an individual who has received an organ transplant and who runs the danger of having the body reject the organ.

To return to Mallinson (1975), he believes that nations and their educational systems must necessarily evolve to address the needs of the society they are attempting to serve. He cites the factors that affect change (or transformation) in national character (e.g., use of technology and curricular priorities) as the following, which are reminiscent of Appadurai (ed. Featherstone 1990):

- Competition from more progressive groups and the struggle for survival
- Scientific progress and discovery
- The gradual spreading and acceptance of new beliefs that eventually result in a new outlook
- Education has only an indirect influence in that it acts on the intellectual quality of the group rather than directly on its character

Mallinson sees these factors from the view that the nation is still in control of the outcome. If we focus fleetingly on each aspect listed above, however, we can readily see societies dealing with these situations, but no longer solely for the national good (Spring 1998). We also see that competition has forced both business and government to look past national boundaries in favor of maintaining business profitability. Scientific and technological developments within the communication and transportation industries have brought the world to many people's doorstep, in effect destroying the insular capabilities of national boundaries. In other words, these boundaries are no longer an effective means of preventing outside political or cultural influences from infiltrating the national culture. And although education was once perceived as a force that directly influenced the political or cultural makeup of a country, it is now in danger of becoming an indirect or subordinate influence. The possible outcome then is that education would be forced to become an instrument of purely academic concerns. In turn, the learner's nonacademic development would be left to the sometimes chaotic and conflicting cultural flows expressed earlier (Appadurai 1983). This conclusion can already be observed in any educational environment where teachers and administrators are constantly being challenged by these outside forces.

The argument being posited is that education at a national level must meet the demands of the society in which it finds itself. In the past, nationalism may have been the focal point to guarantee the survival of the nation; however, it is no longer certain whether this focus is still critical to most of the world's nations today. An example that comes to mind is China and its ongoing friction with information access on the Internet. In addition, the different types of nationalism may afford a narrowness of thinking that in turn does not cater to the needs of the learner. In the end, the latter must be able to function effectively in an increasingly global context. From this view it becomes apparent that for education to become an effective socializing instrument, it must look for a new perspective.

To be fair to Mallinson, he does speculate that, considering the direction he sees society going, there is only one eventual outcome for education, which he labels as **transnationalism** (Mallinson 1975). Why he said this bears further investigation, and we will analyze it further in the next section.

The underlying significance of this analysis, however, should not be lost. It suggests that we are living in a world where national borders appear to be playing an increasingly secondary role in one's life. Although individuals today may not consciously consider their international situation, it is very likely that they experience unprecedented undercurrents that would encourage them to use words like **international**, **multinational**, **transnational**, **global village**, world, etc. In effect, most individuals currently label events that affect them within a much broader global framework.

With this in mind, it is time to address more accurately those labels that achieve a higher importance in this shifting social paradigm. The next section therefore will focus on exploring related concepts and their relevance to the educational environment of contemporary society.

"INTERNATIONAL," "GLOBAL," AND "UNIVERSAL" AS SIGNIFIERS FOR EDUCATION

Despite the fact that our discussion primarily centers on public education in western society, we would be remiss not to give some discussion to issues confronting education at the world level. We find there is a distinct need to address those changes that are contributing to our twenty-first-century society, at least in terms of information accessibility and availability. Indeed, if one were to refer to an idea, concept or perspective as being "global," then it becomes "very sexy"—something which has strong appeal and about which everyone apparently has some idea. However, if we are to truly understand the educational environment, then we must at least contemplate these labels that are bandied about with little or no regard.

Education, especially, is not immune to the attraction of a global perspective, and perhaps for very good reason. Because a school prepares students with the skills they'll need to be successful, we can argue that it is a socializing process for the "global" environment. By the same token, however, education has the potential to provide an equally strong model for any change patterns that are considered vital for an educational process. Those patterns would be based on the ideological focus of that particular society—that of perhaps a "global" versus an "international" framework.

Interestingly, if one were to assume that globalization and internationalism were one and the same, then the role of education, as specified above, becomes doubtful: the implications of globalization as opposed to those that support an international perspective, will ultimately dictate priorities for any curriculum that educators may develop and implement. While the notion of the world as a "global village" conjures up notions of warmth and togetherness, it may not be to everyone's liking. There are a number of very good reasons for this, not the least of which are the potentially unsavory answers to the questions: Who will pay the bills? Who will be in charge? And who will run the village? While these questions may appear initially flippant, these areas still bear further enquiry. Jones (Jones 1998) outlines what Waters (Waters 1995) first stated, which was then organized by Little (1996), into the "ideal-typical patterns" of globalization along the following lines:

- Economic globalization
- Political globalization
- Cultural globalization

According to Jones, these are the three areas of globalization that best summarize what is occurring in the world, and he believes that the process of globalization can be explained through this level of deconstruction. This analysis brings to light very important implications which appear to be inherent to the process of our social development, and since education is a reflection of the society it was meant to serve (see Chapter 3 and Chapter 6), it may help us to focus on the choices educators should make. An "international education" which this author believes should have its home in all arenas of education (public, private, and international) would better serve as a descriptor for an educational program that encourages an "international understanding." Vyas (*UNESCO Projects on International Understanding and Peace* 1983), in his book on UNESCO contributions to education, describes how important it is that learners understand their place in the world to better inform their outlook on their own lives. Briefly, this would entail developing a perspective that allows students to internalize the connections between themselves, as individuals, and the rest of the world. This view opposes the perhaps less attentive globalist or nationalist agenda, an agenda that is perhaps much more comfortable with maintaining the status quo as its primary focus. Unfortunately, a visit to any particular academic setting immediately provides evidence that homogeneity in all its forms and guises is no longer a valid concept—save for, perhaps, curricular programs and teaching methodologies, both of which are historically referenced (see chapters 15 and 16 on Second-Order Change).

The term "globalization" may have more hegemonic roots to its ideology than the term internationalism. We can argue that the very notion of creating a global economy within the global village is in fact an extension of the hegemonic practices of the great modern imperial powers. The global economy appears to have begun when these imperial powers began to colonize other parts of the world. The globalization that has continued since that time is simply an extension of the "cultural imperialistic paradigm" (Spring, 1998).

There has also been speculation that the sudden rise in the popularity of the so-called "international school" after World War II may have been a direct result of a political decision by the war's victorious powers. It may also have been due to threats from the nuclear age. In any case, it appears that Jones outlines what has become the norm: the trend of dominance through war and displacement has shifted to a more subtle form of hegemony via economic, political and cultural means (e.g. the European Union, Free Trade agreements, and multinational corporations). This in turn could mean a potential loss of cultural diversity in favor of one homogeneous world culture, possibly because of the needed uniformity for the different globalization patterns, as argued earlier (Appadurai, 1983).

While some may argue that this process of cultural homogeneity is inevitable, it is this author's belief that the apparently sudden sociopolitical changes brought about by mass immigration, technological innovation, and changing social patterns is wreaking havoc on the modernist conventions of mass education. This is perhaps the crux of why public education finds itself in this vicious spiral of playing catch-up to society. It is also the crux of the reason why education must rethink itself, so that it could provide a sustainable and meaningful educational model for our society. Perhaps part of this needed shift may incorporate a culture of what Vyas calls "international understanding" (*UNESCO Projects on International Understanding and Peace*, 1983). To summarize Vyas' stance, the main focus in expressing the need for an "international understanding" would be to create and develop an attitude among all educational parties that would help facilitate relations between people from different national backgrounds or cultures. Vyas states that this understanding will occur when the home culture is maintained and encouraged while at the same time an attempt would be made by these same educational parties to positively understand and interact transformatively (see Chapter 10) with other cultures.

It now remains to determine where the impetus for this "international understanding" should lie within the educational environment. It is possible that the answer is already available. Kurt Hahn believed it was more important to create an "international awareness" (which can be argued as being a precursor to Vyas' "international understanding") in the child than to create a comprehensive academic background (Cambridge 2001). Roger Peel, the former director of the International Baccalaureate Organization, provides an example which may prove fruitful for public education. He believed that the paradigm for the IB curricular programme (see Chapter 4) was shifting from "a curriculum for international schools to an international curriculum for schools" (Wallace 1997). If we adopt this perspective and combine it with the thoughts of Mattern and Matthews (see Chapter 4), it becomes easier to see that the probable key to being able to apply Hahn's initial "awareness" and Vyas's "international understanding" would be in embedding these two aspects into the curricula and teaching methodologies of every educational institution.

A CLOSER LOOK AT THE WORD "INTERNATIONAL" AND ITS IMPLICATIONS FOR EDUCATION

The word international is being used more extensively in today's educational vocabulary. Even within higher academic contexts, the word has at least two meanings. The first meaning deals with international education in a comparative educational context, implying education's concern with developing countries and their respective national education systems (Crossley and Broadfoot 1992). According to this meaning, the focus is largely on practical, problem-solving issues, and it has strong ties with development agencies such as the World Bank (Jones 1995).

Interestingly, there is also a parallel development in education that has been labeled as "international education." This particular facet dealt initially with the education of children within an "international" community, when the children's parents have taken up residence in another land for occupational purposes. Within this meaning, an international education is largely associated with the "international schools" those children attend (Zsebik 2003). For the most part, these schools are populated by a small segment of society. While the system of international education is of interest in itself, in this context it serves only as a beginning point for our discussion. To proceed further, therefore, we will have to break down our concept of what the word international implies, to more fully comprehend what it means for public education.

Various resources use interesting notions to define international. We shall begin with the simplest of these resources, the dictionary (Thompson 1995). The definition for international reads thus: "existing, involving, or carried on between two or more nations."

If we pursue this line of analysis further, we find the word international thus defined in McLeish (*Key Ideas in Human Thought 1995*):

> The real meaning (from an etymological point of view) of international is "inter-state": that is, relationships between states, rather than nations—thus 'internationalism', properly employed, should express solidarity and equality among nations rather than states (McLeish 1995).

This idea from McLeish bears some significance. Here he clearly demonstrates a distinction between the nation, as defined by the geographical boundaries which limit the state, and the nation as a community of individuals who share the feeling of belonging to a group united by common racial, linguistic, and historical ties.

However, when the concept of international is applied to a real, political world, its context is established as focusing on sovereign territories. As an example, Carder (1998) outlines that the tensions between Iraq and the United Nations unleashed the following perception:

> Iraq must "comply with the will of the international community" (New sanctions on Iraq—November 13, 1997). This puts "international" and mainly "international community" in a new light. It is the body in today's world which has ultimate power and must be obeyed (Carder 1998).

Carder's interpretation implies that the way the international community (which in this case is comprised of sovereign geographical areas) uses the term international, determines international decision making, and that nations are now accountable to the community they belong to. While Carder's interpretation still leaves room to speculate on what exactly constitutes an international community, it does not explain at what level these international decisions will be applied. The general sense is that members of the international community constantly interact in an effort to either better their position or, in case of a conflict, to be responsible for their actions. Recent events in Afghanistan, and now again in Iraq, have also provided strong evidence that the international community can be a decisive force in world politics, and that violating a country's sovereignty is now acceptable if it is for the "greater good" of this international community.

From a purely linguistic perspective, however, breaking the word down into its composite parts (i.e. inter-national) provides some insight as to its most appropriate usage. The prefix "inter" implies a merging of two (or more) separate bodies to create a common link—common vernacular points to this concept. Thus international implies a relationship between two separate nations for the purpose of interaction.

From the above we can gather that there are two separate notions concerning international. One focuses on the interaction of states while the other focuses on the interaction of different cultural groups that are not necessarily defined by a sovereign territory.

It is now necessary to briefly return to the idea of 'international education' to help determine which context appears to be more applicable for public education. It is important to see in this particular discussion that the idea of "nation" is attached to a specific culture, while "state" is attached to a specific geographical location as described above. In other words, nations are created through an interactive process of the entire community while the idea of state is created through political decision making practices which may or may not be independent of the national cultural makeup of the people it affects (Zsebik, 2003).

To summarize therefore, the word international for our purpose has taken the following forms:

- Existing, involving, or carried on between two or more nations
- The prefix "inter" in international implies a merging of two separate bodies to create a common link.

Thus the term international can be construed as

> a situation where two or more nations or cultures (not states) come together for the purpose of interacting to produce positive common links that express solidarity and equality between those involved.

Returning once more to the library reference section, we find an entry within the Fontana Dictionary (Bullock 1988) for "international education":

> International education...appears to be a reflection of the emergence of international economic, political, and cultural linkages leading towards what some claim is an emergent global social system....The goal of international education is the development of a cognitive awareness (some would claim affective and behavioural corollaries) of the international dimensions of economy, polity, society, culture, aesthetics, etc.

This above definition brings about an interesting notion that though individuals within the international community may initially have very little in common with each other, common features do exist as evidenced in the listed dimensions of economy, polity, society, culture, aesthetics, etc. The definition also creates the perspective that an international education develops an international awareness (and perhaps understanding, Vyas, 1983) of the global society in which the student is (or will be) taking part. This serves to strengthen the concept that an "international education" is not simply a national education in an overseas setting, but rather an educational prospect that promotes the ideas of "an international awareness," or "education for international understanding". This is also seen through such publications from UNESCO (*Guiding Principles Relating to Education for International Understanding* 1968), and "worldmindedness" (Sampson & Smith, 1957, taken from Hayden & Thompson, 1995) through community linkages. From the research, it appears that there is already a connection between globalization and its apparent need for an international understanding that creates a perspective of worldmindedness.

From this standpoint, it becomes clear that institutions which solely carry the word international in their name, but which don't actually promote an international *understanding* through communal interaction, may not be fulfilling the requirements that an international education entails. It also becomes clear that if public education is to maintain its relevancy for our contemporary, postmodern, technologically oriented society, then it, too, must take the concept of worldly-mindedness seriously.

A Closer Look at the Word "Globalization" and Its Implications for Education

In the course of developing a cohesive argument, it is necessary to try to illuminate this particular premise defined as globalization. De Alba et al. (2000) apparently realize this necessity and make an attempt to classify globalization as something that results in a people, country, or group of countries or regions being impacted by the effects of situations produced within specific sites in the world. This situation is generated in the most diverse conditions and parts of the world, within specific sites that can be more or less near or distant to others geographically, politically, or culturally and whose effects on the people, country or group of countries are located in the interrelationship among these geographic, political, or cultural elements (de Alba et al. 2000).

De Alba et al. continue with the notion that globalization has many facets which include finance, scientific and technological advances, information and the media, trade and transportation, minorities and majorities, migratory movements, democracy and participation, human rights, and the issue of gender. Each one of these areas listed above have in one way or another led to the creation and development of this globalization process.

The facets outlined by de Alba also can be closely connected to the global cultural flows, previously outlined by Appadurai (ed. Featherstone 1993), who sees certain global trends as fluid movements between different areas of the world. Those movements affect the overall development of globalization.

Jones (1998) points to globalization as an economic process, "which starts with its most obvious and fundamental feature—the organization and integration of economic activity at levels which transcend national borders and jurisdictions." From there, however, Jones points out the necessity of extending the concept of the globalization process "beyond a straightforward reductionist view of economic integration," to a view that was first expressed by Hall (1991a, b) as

> an emphasis on how the global articulates with the local and upon a view of globalization that recognizes the inevitability of persistent multiplicity and diversity among cultures rather than the inevitability of bland homogenization. Adopting a bottom-up view of globalization is necessary, claimed Hall (1991a) if we are to avoid the simplicity of a reductionist view of globalization as "monolithic, noncontradictory, (and) uncontested."

It is this last quotation that perhaps clarifies the danger education faces when it attempts to determine its future philosophical orientation. While it seems there is little apparent need for public education to possess an international mindset, in fact the argument is that an international perspective in the public education environment may better serve its goals of preparing students for the future.

This is particularly pertinent when we are concerned with "education in an international context" as opposed to an "international education." It is the premise of this author that an education in an international context carries a greater possibility of experiencing the above-mentioned "monolithic, non-contradictory, (and) uncontested" agenda that Jones and Hall suggested. On the other hand, if treated with the proper philosophical grounding, an international education provides more impetus towards maintaining this "persistent multiplicity and diversity among cultures." In other words, it carries an inherent bias towards the idea of the international *understanding* cited previously. This bias is necessary for a *true* international education to occur. Without this bias of cultural diversity, we risk reducing or losing many important teaching opportunities. Additionally, a status quo school environment that focuses on the idea of developing a good worker in a globalized setting would not take the complexity of today's world into account, and may therefore not teach the necessary skills to children who will have to live in that world.

Jones concedes that it is still necessary to have some sort of organizational strategy to maintain the globalization process In the following quote, he states that this strategy would come from existing national governing bodies:

> I do not join those who see in globalization the collapse of the state or the erosion of governmental participation in economic life. On the contrary, the logic of globalization implies the active involvement of state mechanisms in order to ensure the unfettered operation of markets, both capital and labor ...One of the ironies of globalization is its reliance on the state to make possible the free operation of markets... (ibid.)

In other words, Jones realizes that there has to be an overture made to the different layers of systemic organization to create a sense of community for globalization. If this is the case, however, then it becomes clearer that this process of globalization only strengthens the argument that the mandate for education should be focused toward an "international education," even within the various national educational environments. This international education would focus on developing the skills necessary for interaction within and between the different levels of community. The final outcome would be achieving an "international understanding" within the student.

Held et al. (*Global Transformations, Politics, Economics, and Culture* 1999) take the viewpoint that globalization cannot be described as a "single discreet phenomenon," but rather, that there are three contrasting currents or views which can be identified: "the hyperglobalist, the skeptical, and the transformationalist." He outlines each viewpoint as follows:

The Hyperglobalist Thesis

For the hyperglobalisers, history and economics have come together at the end of the twentieth century to create a new order of relations in which states are either converging economically and politically, or are being made irrelevant by the activities of transnational business ...Yet this view (for an international education), is also ambiguous and apolitical because various critics of the hyperglobalist thesis argue either that it is an apology for the current dominance of neo-liberal free market capitalism, on the one hand, or for the spread of social democratic regulation of markets, on the other...

Skeptical Thesis

Skeptics argue that "historical evidence indicates the world is not becoming a single market, but that it is the development of regional economic blocks and facilitation of trade between countries which has extended..." Against this analysis, the development of international schools as outposts of other national cultures and the development of international education as encapsulated outposts of "other" national cultures, and the development of international education, can be interpreted as pragmatic responses to economic circumstances where a school that serves a single national grouping is unviable.

Transformationalist Thesis

To adherents of the transformationalist thesis of globalization, reference to the economic marginalization of whole countries is unjustifiable, since "the familiar core-periphery hierarchy is no longer a geographic but a social division of the world economy...North and South, First World and Third World are no longer "out there" but nestled within all the world's major cities" (Held et al 1999).

If we combine the experiences and interactions of "international understanding," we find that we can devise a structure that demonstrates a **continuum of interaction**. This interaction would span from individual interaction (the micro-culture) to a more universal construct that expands to include the sum total of all interactions in the educational environment. This then in turn defines the qualities of civilization (see Fig. 7.1). By the same token, if individuals become aware of the other layers in the continuum, they would have better decision-making capabilities throughout every level of interaction. In other words, an awareness of the interaction between these different layers would improve students' overall perspective of the individual places they hold in society. This awareness would result in an intellectual perspective of a transformative nature (see Chapters 10 and 11), which would range from a local perspective (that focuses on the student's own culture and character) to an international perspective (that focuses on the process of globalization combined with the need to understand and be aware of an international nature). To understand Figure 7.1 shown below, it is important to remember the following:

- Each layer builds on the other, resulting in change or decision for the individual through the global levels
- The process is continuous
- The layers which the individual can perceive contribute to that individual's world view on a daily basis
- Every individual makes a contribution to the society with which he or she interacts

There is no conflict of interest between a local and a global orientation. It can be seen as part of an interrelated connection between the individual and the role that each individual plays within each of the social layers. Education will play a pivotal role in determining individual learning throughout this continuum And the optimal result would be to maintain cultural diversity. At the same time, education must acknowledge the student's responsibility within this continuum.

In order for this focus to be effective, the educational outcome must have well-defined parameters encompassing a perspective that ranges from micro through macro. With this in mind, it becomes clearer that an education which focuses on students' international awareness and their understanding of their individual relationships to larger society would be the most appropriate direction for education within any context. This direction would satisfy the premise of promoting an "international education."

The question then remains: How can educators function in a global environment and produce a formal curriculum which bears relevance to that society? Perhaps it is necessary to focus on common or universal elements which could lead towards that goal: creating an academic structure that provides enough relevant scope to both a local and a global orientation.

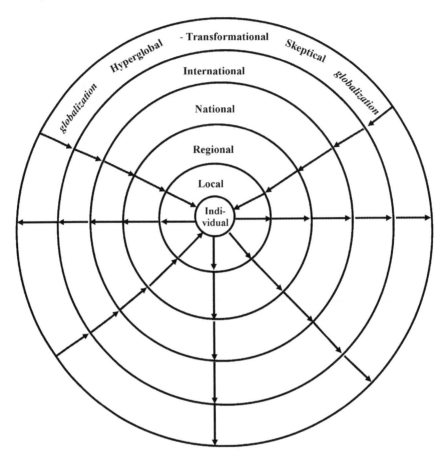

FIG 7.1 *A simplified representation of society and the continuum of two-way interaction between the individual through to the global community*

A Closer Look at the Word "Universal" and Its Implications for Education

As we continue to pursue the impact of globalization on education, we will examine an educational perspective of the different processes that occur in society. One approach may be to delve into what may be considered universal. What can be considered as common among all the peoples of the world?

At first it may appear that this line of thought would be difficult to justify if one were to try to find common ground in a world riddled with conflict. It could be argued, however, that common features do exist. Perhaps the most obvious is that the human race is of one species, and while this seems an obvious statement, it still bears some reflection considering the ongoing issues related to prejudice and discrimination. Ironically, the latter may also be construed as a common feature, and though that feature takes a negative form, it does strengthen the argument that commonalities can exist.

This author believes there is a need to follow a back-to-basics concept for education. This is not to say that we need to return to the three Rs (Reading, wRiting, and aRithmetic—the author's emphasis) of an earlier educational era, but rather, our focus is to determine what constitutes the human species. In other words, perhaps education's mandate to serve the needs of the society in which it is to be found, dictates that we need to look past all the created or constructed differences, whether those are academic or social; we need to attempt a deconstruction to find anything that we can deem as generally beneficial to society. Once we become familiar with this orientation, then it becomes a matter of determining the educational aims necessary to satisfy a positive educational outcome for each point within a universal continuum of knowledge acquisition and development (see Figure 7.2 below). Current educational programs found within the western didactic have these particular aims in mind, but the question is to what extent they have been successful in this area. If they are designed according to these notions listed above, then these curricular structures are set to lead education into the next century. If not, then it will prove necessary to search for educational alternatives that offer a two-pronged approach—one that helps students know their own culture while demonstrating their individual relationship to others at different levels of the continuum (see Fig 7.2 below). This approach is especially necessary within the ideological realm of a public institution that claims to engender a contemporary sociopolitical ideology.

As can be seen, concepts like global and international and their derivations have encroached on the common vernacular, both within society and in education. This trend strongly implies the direction in which society is heading; yet at the same time, there is little guidance that establishes how public education should proceed.

To complete our vocabulary tour, we need to account for one more term that may prove to be productive for education: the term universal. A curriculum that has a universal basis and that's derived from elements of the human condition does not imply the creation of a hegemonic environment. Rather, such a curriculum would serve to provide a basis from which to derive all other educational experiences. This would create cohesiveness throughout the educational environment, which would result in enhanced understanding, not only of the sociohistorical backdrop of globalization as described above, but also of a students' own future orientation which can help them determine their place in that society. While this particular concept may strike the reader as radical, it is not new to educational research as demonstrated in the following paragraphs, thereby lending further credibility to efforts in this direction.

Feldman (1980) suggests that the "developmental psychology of intelligence has preoccupied itself with the study of universals; the achievements which we all will accomplish...those qualities that make us a part of the human family, by showing that we will all share certain experiences of growth and change ... (and the focus on universals) has done its part to help transcend bigotry, prejudice, and petty differences among individuals and groups.'

Feldman continues by outlining the idea of *Universal Achievement:*

> It has been the major purpose of Piaget's empirical work, for example, to document the common achievements eventually attained by all individuals in all cultures. Piaget and his coworkers have thus attempted to isolate

and describe those qualities that make us all cognitively part of the human family (ibid.).

He then proceeds to outline the concept of *Universal Conditions*:

> The environmental conditions that help to stimulate the acquisition of universal bodies of knowledge seem to be of two types: human conditions and non-human ones. An example of a non-human universal condition is the redundancy present in the physical environment which leads the child to discover that the world consists of permanent, three-dimensional objects...human conditions include internal qualities of the changing individual as well as conditions created by social interaction with others (ibid.).

These factors which Feldman has outlined are important in that they demonstrate some orientation when applying the term universal to education. His work implies a conscious decision to invoke the term universal as it applies to oneness—an implication that terms like "global" or "world" does not cover. In other words, the foundation for exploring cultural diversity around the world needs to focus on the commonality of humanity's needs as a foundation for the exploration of the world's cultural diversity

To put it simply, the term universal may be a better philosophical basis in an educational format that aims at producing "citizens of the world" who can function in "inter-national" contexts. It would in effect help to define an academic environment that would promote the "pan-nationalism" outlined by McKenzie , who has indicated this concept as needing to be "underpinned ... by a set of values congruent with the drive for international understanding" (McKenzie 1998). Interestingly, the idea of international understanding echoes Vyas's insight (1983) mentioned earlier. Accomplishing this international understanding would require creating a basis from which to determine and deliver curricular material that's relevant to the suggested academic environment.

The term universal is also appealing because of its association with other existing educational enterprises. The United Nations is perhaps the most prominent example in the collective societal conscious whose aim is to idealistically demonstrate the universality of our species. From this organization stems such examples as the Universal Declaration of Human Rights and the Universal Rights of the Child. These contributions appear to demonstrate a need to focus on finding some common elements which would enable individuals to live together in peace. The use of the term universal in an educational context, therefore, could be construed as a logical extension of the ideology behind these other contributions.

Feldman (1980) brings out one last perspective to consider. Feldman takes the idea of universals, as he has described above, and places them on a learning continuum (see Fig. 7.2 below) which he believes more accurately reflects the learning process of a child. To summarize, a new idea begins its academic life as a "novelty" piece of knowledge. If accepted as "novelty," then that knowledge becomes unique.

At this stage, the individual has to decide whether the knowledge which has gained the status of "unique" is useful. If it is not, then the knowledge is labeled as "noncreative." Feldman defines noncreative as meaning that "a particular novelty, however unusual, daring, expressive, satisfying or individually meaningful, does not contribute in any significant way to another's understanding of a field." If, however, the knowledge does appear to be useful to the society in question, then it proceeds along the learning continuum until it becomes universal in its acceptance. This concept can apply to the knowledge we acquire in all areas, be it factual, abstract, discipline-related, or culturally based in nature.

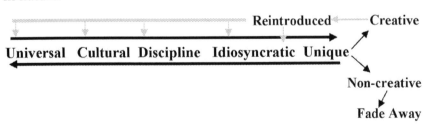

Fig 7.2 – *The unique to universal continuum (black arrow line) illustrating extension of a domain after creative organization (Feldman) with enhancement by author of functionality in both directions (gray arrow line) and reintroduction of creative thought through learning.*

Children go through the process described in Fig 7.2 with great regularity. For instance, their curiosity is awakened if they are confronted with a piece of wood (the violin) that's cut in strange shapes and has four pieces of wire stretched across the front. They have entered the field of "novelty." At this point, if they were to experience nothing more that is related to this strange contraption, then they would abandon it and lose interest.

Enter the educator who demonstrates the potential uses of this wooden contraption. Now the children are experiencing its use and perhaps the benefits of this device; they begin the educational journey of discovery where they find out how to manipulate it, how to master it, its importance, and eventually, its universal nature. Taken in reverse, the violin, which has become a "universal" within the child's mind, can now lead in the other direction. It becomes a unique musical product which has relevance to the cultural, disciplinary, and idiosyncratic knowledge base that's relevant to the instrument. If it appeals to the listener, it will be labeled "creative" and the performance will be repeated; if not it will be labeled "noncreative" and discarded. The signifying word, universal in this case indicates that this signifier applies to concepts or elements which become immediately recognizable once the initial model or formula has been demonstrated. This signification, as we will see, can serve in different capacities, be it when describing a physical object or an abstract concept.

It is important to note that the idea of teaching along Feldman's continuum can be extended into the sociopolitical domain whereby the universal features of our human race can be incorporated and then broken down into their component parts. This process helps students learn what makes them unique as individuals. At the same time, concepts which may appear to be unique (or a "novelty") to the student can be brought back to a level of universality, if that outcome is intended. It is important that educators keep this two-way process in mind. In order for a universal concept to be addressed and accepted into the constructs of the student's awareness, it must be deconstructed to a unique level. By the same token, a unique concept should be carried forward to determine its universal level of agreement. Working in this direction does not necessarily mean the loss of uniqueness, but rather it expresses to what extent this uniqueness extends along the continuum towards the universal end of the spectrum.

Interestingly, we begin to see a direction in curricular development which could satisfy the construction and deconstruction process posed above for our developmental continuum of society, ranging from the individual to the universal. In other words, this concept of "unique-to-universal" or "universal-to-unique" may point to a new way of organizing an educational environment so that the idea of a universal skill or knowledge base could be identified for the teacher and achieved by the learner.

From an "international educational" perspective in today's society, it would seem more appropriate to attempt a paradigmatic shift which places emphasis on the oneness and uniqueness of humankind while still encouraging exploration of cultural differences, instead of the hegemonic constructs of a monocultural educational orientation.

This would not mean the eradication of one's own culture or one's own personality, but rather, as demonstrated above with Feldman's continuum, to incorporate the notion of the universal human nature into the other levels of an individual's educational experience. This notion would be in keeping with other attempts to provide an intimation towards a universal construct such as the Universal Declaration of Human Rights, the Universal Rights of the Child, and more recently, the Chicago Declaration towards a Global Ethic (Küng 1998).

There is a quite simple connection between this universal concept of education, that of globalization, and the experience of a true "international education": a curriculum with a universal basis and an international perspective could provide a solid foundation from which all other academic exercises would spring. To have a universal basis would help to guarantee that students are aware of the acculturation processes within their academic environment and how this environment affects them throughout the continuum. One of the major goals of an "international educational perspective" therefore would be to develop in the student not only a multicultural perspective that will prevent a global reductionist view of the world but also an equally strong perspective of the student's individual place in the world (a local viewpoint). This would be accomplished within the student's own culture through active involvement and participation with other cultures, and through developing the life skills that are necessary for students to participate effectively in this "new world order." In other words, the focus will be on promoting an international "perspective" or "awareness," the main thrust of which would be to develop individual skills for positive interaction between people of different nations and cultures.

From all vantages, it appears that the concept of a "universal basis" for public education should focus on developing an educational paradigm that addresses our contemporary, postmodern "global village" society. Incorporating this universal nature to the curriculum would provide a framework from which to choose a future course as an alternative to historically referenced models of curricular programming. We now have to decide whether the curricular structures that currently provide the bulk of program choice in public education warrant the label of a progressive sociopolitical curricular framework—one that contributes to the overall creation of an appropriate educational dialectic for our current society. The latter would be accomplished by incorporating constructs common to all in the global community.

DISCUSSION AND REVIEW QUESTIONS FOR CHAPTER 7

1. Why would knowledge of what goes on outside of your particular educational environment prove helpful?

2. What are some of the ideological perspectives that appear to be inherent in public education? Why were they adopted? Which current events in the world could change these ideological perspectives? Create a table that allows comparison of these ideological perspectives.

3. Describe some of the challenges that may arise if public education is restructured to better align with the changes in contemporary society.

4. Describe some of the opportunities that may arise for education in this contemporary context. Are they feasible? Why or why not?

5. How does the notion of an "international education" help public education?

6. Discuss how the final definition of an "international education" could benefit public education within a national context.

7. Outline the argument for an international mindset for education as it pertains to a national environment. Do you agree? Why or why not?

8. Discuss which *theses* (e.g. Hyper-globalist, Sceptical, Transformationalist) you believe is the most appropriate for describing our current socio-political environment.

9. Outline the implications that the label *universal* has on public education. How can a universal notion for education

be justified in the context of the current socio-political framework?

10. Create a concrete example from your experience for Feldman's unique-to-universal continuum. What does this imply for education in general?

11. Discuss the benefits of a universal perspective for education. How would this inform one's own practices?

Chapter 8

Aligning Public Education to Contemporary Society

In previous chapters, we have been exploring what comprises an educational environment and what comprises a social environment. In an effort to create a more favorable setting for education in the twenty-first century, we must now merge these two areas. To begin this process, we must turn our attention to the physical location of this merging—the public school.

A public school is defined by the daily activities and people occupying the physical space we label as "school." The majority of schools consist of different elements that, to varying degrees, influence the school environment; these elements come in the form of students, parents, administration, curriculum, and educators. In effect, the interaction between these individuals who have come together to take part in the act of educating through an agreed-upon curricular program have formed a community which would not otherwise have been formed (see Chapter 12).

Does the presence of a culturally diverse community in a public school necessarily mean that an international state of mind must be given priority? If there is common agreement that the prime reason for the existence of this school is to prepare learners for success in the greater community—one that is completely saturated with multicultural and international influences—then one would hope that the answer would be a resounding yes.

Where there is a diversity of culture and perspectives, a need to have some common focus arises. This may not be present within the mandated curriculum, which oftentimes exclusively focuses on the formal or academic curriculum. There is, however, a danger of using the formal curriculum as the basis for this common focus. Doing this may prevent an institution from addressing other issues that may be of equal or greater import for the school environment. Yes, there may be academic institutions that are adept at creating the right balance to prepare their students, not only for further studies, but also for the sociopolitical environment in which they will live. However, it can be equally safe to assume that there are academic institutions which may find themselves in need of additional guidance to help them fulfill their mandated policies. Indeed, enacting policies that encourage ideological, sociological, and philosophical perspectives that are in line with the society in which these institutions reside takes a great deal of inspiration, understanding, courage and conviction. Therefore, the next action is to provide a feasible framework that helps clarify a public school's areas of need.

DEVELOPING THE DIAGNOSTIC ANALYSIS FURTHER

If we accept the notion that public education should understand the different sociopolitical pressures in our society if we acknowledge the need to create an international perspective in public education, and if we apply this perspective to the school to better meet the needs of our society, then we are faced with the following proposition:

> *A school's sociopolitical environment may be considered relevant to the society it is meant to serve when individuals in that environment learn to interact and produce common links that express solidarity and equality of nations or cultures (not states). This is accomplished through positive participation with peers and other outside influences.*

Is this currently the case?

The answer is doubtful, particularly when we question the origin of the curriculum, the nationalistic traditions and backgrounds of the teaching staff, and the general nature of prevailing attitudes and biases within the institution. The difficulty is that educators may inadvertently work within the assumptions inherent in their cultural construct. Langford (1998), however, reminds us of the ever-increasing numbers of children whom she refers to as "global nomads." These are children who

> have grown up in foreign countries, (but) they are not integral parts of those countries. When they come to their country of citizenship (some for the first time), they do not feel at home, because they do not know the lingo or expectations of others...Where they feel most like themselves is in that interstitial culture, which is created, shared and carried by persons who are relating societies, or sections thereof, to each other (Useem 1976 as cited in Langford 1998).

In addition, Langford then quotes Pollock in Killham (see Langford 1998) as stating that "the Global Nomad of today is the prototype of the citizen of the twenty-first century." Indeed, although there are still sizable pockets of homogeneity in public education, we can safely assume that rising immigration rates and increased mobility in society will reduce homogeneity. From this perspective, we cannot argue that the school is serving the community merely because it is filled with members of that community. Neither can an education environment justify a similar line of argument based solely on a mission statement or philosophy encouraging elements such as inclusivity but little else. There has to be more in our philosophical justification for what we do in public education.

The implications of this viewpoint for public education are enormous. It appears that we can no longer justify continuing to offer a curricular structure that offers a particular national perspective. It also appears that we cannot call certain schools relevant simply because of the multicultural makeup of the student body. This particular frame of reference provides no guidance or support to a student who is challenged by the school environment. A struggle within the environment may also ensue between what is being promoted as a "multicultural environment" and what is really occurring in that environment, perhaps with a bias that may not be the most appropriate for today's society. We may also need to question the cultural *outlook* (not background) of the teaching body, along with other aspects of the school, to determine if it promotes the appropriate international perspective. In this case the focus would optimally be on promoting a culture of "global citizenship," through developing a critical understanding of internationalism and its relationships within this global society. It is hoped these ideas will provoke new questions and open up new areas of discussion.

REVISITING OUR SOCIOPOLITICAL SYSTEMS – APPLYING THESE TERMS TO EDUCATION

As can be seen from Chapter 7, the term international holds three distinct variations that are easily identified:

- In the first place, an international education is concerned with issues of an economic and developmental purpose, and it is usually tied to the World Bank and other economic developmental organizations. There are strong ties to nongovernmental agencies that are in the business of developing educational services that help developing countries grow economically—perhaps with an imperialistic or hegemonic price tag attached.

- In the second place, an international education is concerned with the education of children whose parents live and work overseas. In this case, there may be an isolationist or hegemonic price tag attached.

- In the third, and perhaps most important place, an international education within a public institutional setting has the potential to push public education closer to an alignment with our twenty-first-century society that it is intended to service. However, there are possible challenges to overcome as well within this last setting. It has the potential to open a Pandora's box of politicization, self-interest, and mismanagement. The latter could occur if any of the SPACE elements that are in the institutional environment attempt to fulfill their own self-interests, something that public education should not allow.

While the descriptor "multinational" may be valid if the educational environment includes several nationalities or ethnic groups, it nevertheless appears to fall short of a complete application, perhaps because it only serves to describe the fact that several nationalities exist within a specific context. In other words, it is a static description that fails to relate the notion of interaction between the nations—an objective that is far from most current educational ideals. Even from a business perspective, the term multinational implies that it is one company with offices in many countries. If you happen to be the owner of several schools in several countries, then the term may be defensible, but only from a financial perspective. Taken in its entirety, though, this descriptor does not fulfill the philosophical objectives on which we are focusing.

The label "transnational" as an alternative descriptor may find use with those schools promoting a mononational educational culture and who are educating a mononational (monocultural) clientele. Some American schools overseas, for example, may fit into this category. In those schools, the clientele consist exclusively of expatriate American nationals whose children attend a school where (North) American staff teach American curricula. In effect, the school is a clone of a standard U.S. institution that's been transplanted into another country for the sole purpose of educating expatriate U.S. citizens. Even in the public system it is possible to find that adopted curricular programs from other systemic environments have been grafted onto the public system.

Supranational as defined in the dictionary (Thompson 1995) is a term that offers interesting possibilities. The concept of *transcending national limits* has some appeal when in regards to the changing shape of our society of today. It may be that the phrase "supranational school" will, in the not too distant future, be a valid label for an education system if countries continue to amalgamate into trading blocs, if man-made geopolitical divisions cease to exist, and if the globalization process continues unabated. This particular label appears to have much in common with what McKenzie calls Going, Going, Gone...Global!, and Hayden & Thompson (1998) calls "**Pan–national**." "The pan–national works consciously to reduce tensions and misunderstandings across nations by promoting global initiatives, knowledge and empathy through education." (McKenzie 1998). It may also be thought that nongovernmental educational organizations, such as the Advanced Placement (AP), the International Baccalaureate Organization (IBO)—see Chapter 4 for details, and the European Council of International Schools (ECIS) among other NGOs, fit into this category. These supranational educational organizations provide a central service to a large number of schools throughout the world (Thompson 1995a); these schools are nevertheless autonomous from these organizations. In effect, it may be argued that the seeds of a supranational system of schooling have been sown and are awaiting the right moment to provide academic guidance.

DISCUSSION AND REVIEW QUESTIONS FOR CHAPTER 8

1. Discuss to what degree there is a moral imperative for education to prepare learners for the contemporary socio-political environment they will inherit. What does this mean for the other parties involved in the educational process? (Think SPACE Factor.)

2. Utilizing your own experiences, what are some of the institutional challenges that need to be overcome? Frame your response in terms of creating a learning situation that's conducive to today's socio-political environment.

3. What are the implications that arise when considering the need for a relevant curricular program that is servicing our contemporary society?

4. List the different types of international education that can be offered within an educational systemic environment. Draw a comparison table outlining what you perceive as being the similarities and differences from both a philosophical and practical point of view. Write down any conclusions that can be made from your table (see page 96 for any needed clarifications).

5. Read the other types of socio-political structures. Do you see any of these structures as more appropriate for public education? Why?

CHAPTER 9

SOCIAL AND PHILOSOPHICAL INFLUENCES ON EDUCATION

In the past, we have been looking at education with a perspective that can be argued as relying too heavily on its own dialectic. In other words, the system of public education requires itself to understand itself. A position such as this can easily fall prey to using its own traditions and histories to justify its future decisions. The argument being put forward is that accepting the status quo within the education system in actual fact does little to achieving a perspective that may be more appropriate for society's future. Specifically, there is the danger that the logic of current educational arguments are what may termed as circular in orientation; that is the logic contained in the argument is used to justify that argument. All referencing is placed within an enclosed, and in this case habitually traditional frame of reference that may be too rigid too allow other directions in thinking.

That is why throughout our journey we have attempted to reference other areas of inquiry as a means to expanding our understanding of the relationships between education and society. This is done for a purpose; it is to allow some distance from the subject so that when we make conjectures and attempt justification of the arguments being posed, we don't focus exclusively on the system of public education for the answers. In other words, to justify our orientations without taking into consideration the society which public education was meant to serve is at best misplaced and at worst ineffective.

Here then is an overview of the social and pedagogical connections that we can use to help explain this perspective. In the process, we will use critical theory analysis to help explain the vantage being put forward.

DECONSTRUCTING EDUCATION USING STRUCTURALISM

Despite much progress within the social sciences, there appears to be no critical theory that fully explains education's impact on society (and vice versa). In order to better comprehend our current state of public education and its connection to society, we will briefly focus on available social theories, particularly **structuralism**.

In some academic circles, the critical theory of structuralism has acquired the taint of a naughty child, who is not to be discussed in polite society. This reputation is due primarily to the challenges that structuralism presents to more traditional thinkers. The latter consider that the conceptualization of structuralism is too simplistic to be useful in such a complex system as public education. However, structuralism should not be discounted so abruptly as an analytical tool because it allows a novel degree of clarity.

Indeed, the six basic assumptions of structuralism: *wholeness, relationships, de-centering of the subject, self-regulation, dual or synchronous analysis, and transformation* (Gibson, 1984) have much to offer educational enquiry. Before proceeding though, it may be necessary to outline structuralism as a philosophical concept and then to proceed onto its relation to the current theme—that of building a capacity for education in the twenty-first century.

Historically, structuralism has been used by thinkers ranging from Levi-Strauss to deSaussure. It has also been used to help codify or explain a huge variety of subject areas ranging from anthropology to mathematics. Unfortunately for many academic thinkers, its apparent diversity is also cause for alarm, particularly because the term structuralism, lacks a clear definition because of the concept's diverse nature. In addition, some concepts which are inherent in structuralism are, at best, uncomfortable to some. An example is the notion of "de-centering the subject of study" from the focus of attention and placing that subject as only part of the system. This, in turn, has led to an antagonism towards structuralist thought, resulting sometimes in a complete dismissal of any concepts which have been brought to light through its application.

Levi-Strauss, who has been labeled a "universalist" (Sturrock 1979) can be presented as a true structuralist. His complete commitment to using structuralist thought for his analysis of primitive societies is considered to be a standard for structuralist research. Within these analyses, his main focus is the operation of the human mind in *general*, and not just the workings of *particular* minds at particular times. In fact, Levi-Strauss claims to have located a universal mental structure, one which defines the behavior of society in general, although that is being hotly debated even to this day. His other major contribution is in the use of ***binary oppositions*** to help elucidate the sociological situations he confronted. A binary opposition would be two particular elements which, within the society in question, were placed together to help resolve conflicts that might have arisen within that cultural system (e.g., married/not married). These *binary oppositions* were also the impetus for ***transformations*** which occurred within this specific cultural context (Lane 1970). In general, however, the notion of historical significance played neither a major nor a minor role in the analysis.

> For the structuralist, time as a dimension is no less, but no more important than any other that might be used in analysis. History is seen as the specific mode of development of a particular system, whose present, or synchronic nature must be fully known before any account can be given of its evolution, or diachronic nature (Lane 1970).

Notions such as these did not (do not?) endear structuralism to the academic community, as they failed to answer some fundamental questions which are still pervasive enough to warrant consideration. It is, for example, hard to dismiss an individual's personal competence from the sociological equation; this justifies the criticism that structuralist research necessarily limits itself to one particular time and place—a snapshot, if you will.

Interestingly, however, the majority of educators have already had some exposure to structuralism from a number of sources. Perhaps the most famous of these sources is the educational structuralist Piaget. After originally warning about the use of structuralism for analysis in the biological sciences, he later recants and takes the position that organic structures are indeed better explained through a structuralist perspective. Piaget also believes in the need for "decentering" or devaluating the individual. He argues that such a decentering focus will only add to the understanding of the concept in question. In addition, Piaget defends structuralism as a valid concept for education. His work on the learning outcomes and stages of development for a child has now become standard fare for teachers both new and old.

> Attempts to reduce the complex to the simple ... lead to syntheses in which the more basic theory becomes enriched by the derived theory, and the resulting reciprocal assimilation reveals the existence of structures as distinct from additive complexes ... (and this) reduction will not mean impoverishment but such transformation of the two terms connected as benefits both (Piaget 1971).

It is also interesting to note that Piaget paid homage to the individual as a competent human being who has some responsibility for his own actions, but this action is still carried out within the structure that has been outlined as the "system."

> There is ... always a dialectic (*dialogue*) between individual and structure; intelligence develops through interiorized action as the child engages with his world. Piaget's emphasis on construction ... ensures that his work has become the scholarly lynchpin and justification of the progressive tradition of education (Gibson 1984).

This particular line of thought has important implications for individuals who believe a structuralist notion of education bears very little relevance to everyday classroom activity. Rather, structuralism points to a useful direction for understanding and analyzing educational environments which may otherwise prove too unwieldy to observe properly.

Gibson carries these notions further into what can be considered as a form of **neostructuralism**. He proposes "*structural analysis* as a method of studying educational practice with a view to explanation, evaluation and change." This structural analysis which Gibson puts forward is outlined in Figure 9.1. It incorporates structuralist concepts and assumptions, but at the same time, it attempts to remedy some of the "defects" of which structuralism has been accused.

The structural analysis Gibson proposes is comprised of four elements:

- Structures of competence
- Structures of social organization
- Structures of thought
- Structures of feeling

Through these four different structures, social and individual action is realized, constrained and enabled, evidenced and reproduced. The method identifies, through the consideration of actual behavior, those structures which find unique expression as the source and form of individual action (ibid. 1984).

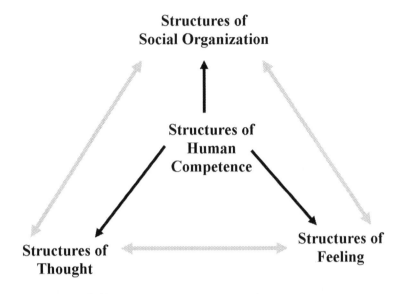

Fig 9.1 – *The Method of Structural Analysis by Gibson*

In other words, an analysis of a social structure considers the individual's competencies as well as including related cultural and historical factors. As an example, when a teacher insists on a certain mode of behavior or a certain line of thinking from the student (e.g., scientific versus creative) then the reasons for this "event" can be analyzed within the social structure in which it is happening. The grounds may be rooted in traditional methods which the teacher has learnt (historical) or in the country the teacher has come from (cultural), or in any number of other factors in the system which may influence the event. In effect, a paradigm has been created within the system. This paradigm is the social construct which dictates the outcome of the event. It is also the driving force for any predetermined decision making throughout the system. If, however, certain pressures or obligations were to be placed on the paradigm currently in place, then the processes of *self-regulation* and, if necessary, *transformation*—two structuralist notions—may shift the paradigm to a more "contemporary" focus. In point of fact, a school or educational authority does indeed go through this process as a reaction to internal or external events. In effect, the school is like a living organism which must daily monitor its "homeostasis" (Piaget 1971) to maintain its internal equilibrium. With this view in mind, Piaget came to the following conclusion:

> If then ... a structure is a systematic whole of self-regulating transformations (educational decision-making and related policies), the organism (the school) is, in a way, the paradigm structure: if we knew our own organism (the school) through and through, it would, on account of its double role of complex physical object and originator of behavior, give us the key to a general theory of structure" (ibid. 1971)—*(Parenthetical comments added to identify relevant elements.)*

In summary, despite Piaget's work on the subject, it may be that a reformed version of structuralist thought, such as the four elements of structure that Gibson proposes, would prove more satisfactory when determining what constitutes an education. We can also analyze the educational paradigm already in place and its implications for society. It is now time to turn our attention to the actual socializing influences affecting today's educational environment.

AN EXPLORATION OF MODERNISM VERSUS POSTMODERNISM

Formal education in western society as we recognize it today grew up in the last one hundred fifty years, over a time in social development where systematic organization, both in physical and abstract terms, led to the development of the then-newly industrialized society (see Chapter 4). This effort placed our civilization at a developmental level that had been unsurpassed in any previously known civilization. Part of the process of development was due to the educational practices which had developed in the era of industrialization. The primary aim of these educational practices was to help the coming generations prepare for the needs of the modern society. Usher and Edwards (1994) have identified several social and historical developments that have affected our own current educational system:

Educational theory and practice is founded on the discourse of modernity and its self-understandings have been forged by that discourse's basic and implicit assumptions. Historically, education can be seen as the vehicle by which modernity's "grand narratives", the Enlightenment ideals of critical reason, individual freedom, progress and benevolent change, are substantiated and realized. The very rationale of the educational process and the role of the educator is founded on modernity's self-motivated, self-directing, rational subject, capable of exercising individual agency (Usher and Edwards 1994).

The last phrase in the above quote requires a response. While it may appear that the idea of individual agency is not a structuralist notion, we can argue that exercising free will still falls within the structure it is intended to serve—in this case, a modernist paradigm. Further, individuals who function within a modernist context will still need to define their actions in the structure of the environment where each person is active, and this definition occurs through the interaction between the individual and the structure itself. Examples range from a doctoral thesis to traffic regulations.

To continue, it is without doubt that both the physical and organizational attributes of any western educational experience is based on modernist theory. Coulby and Jones (1995) neatly trace the expanse of western (European) educational thought. They believe that its origins and related underpinnings were caused by the strict adherence to the "Enlightenment Project," a term used by Coulby and Jones to describe the direction of western thought for the last three hundred to four hundred years. This Enlightenment Project had provided serious direction for the curriculum:

> At school level, almost all (European) countries choose—and the point is that this is a choice—to organize curricular knowledge in the form of subjects, at a more abstruse level, in readily identifiable and distinct cognitive structures...So hegemonic is the epistemology of the subject disciplines that for many graduates and academics it is the only way they can perceive human knowledge to be organized (ibid. 1995).

The argument is that this modernist academic perspective is due to long-held ethnocentric, monocultural, and xenophobic traditions held within European and western academic institutions. In addition, when analyzed more closely, most of the western knowledge base is patriarchal and ethnically white in focus. This biased focus was accomplished through a systematic rejection of the true roots of western thought. Bernal (1987) suggests in Coulby and Jones (1995):

> The ancient model (of thinking) fell not because of any new developments in the field but because it did not fit the prevailing world-view. To be more precise, it was incompatible with the paradigms of race and progress of the early nineteenth century. *(Parentheses added.)*

Bernal instead gives the view that our origins of thought actually came from Egypt and Phoenicia, something which the Greeks themselves were very willing to declare. It wasn't until the Enlightenment Project, which took hold of Europe after the Renaissance, that the importance of this historical fact diminished. Since the Enlightenment, the emphasis was placed almost exclusively on demonstrating a Greek heritage. In point of fact, western academia had succeeded at obscuring nonwestern contributions to human knowledge; it had become an accepted "canon" that knowledge and culture was the exclusive product of one continent: Europe. It can still be argued that nothing has really changed in this particular way of thinking. It may be however that a western-European educational mindset is not the ultimate answer to the creation of a curriculum which fulfills the needed purpose in today's academic environment. It would appear that "Curriculum planners need to be aware of the strand of **cultural relativism** which stresses non-European achievements and influences on knowledge and culture" (Coulby and Jones 1995). Without this awareness, we are apt to propagate a curriculum that continues to maintain the status quo and bears less and less relevance to our postmodern society.

What does postmodernism mean? Research has led to a possible conclusion—that postmodernism is a concept which, by its very nature, rejects the prospect of a clear definition. The closest one could come to framing it would be to state that postmodernism is a social process that has allowed individuals to question the validity of all previous social and cultural dogmas. Once this questioning process has started, the individual or group then assume the responsibility of adopting or creating their own set of norms and values that best fit the new perspective. The result is that previous social models (religion, business, ethics, etc.) have now been jeopardized by a different attitude towards life. The latter can be summarized as follows: *there is no reason why one should conform to something one doesn't agree with if it means giving up the way one chooses to live.*

Usher and Edwards (1994) describe postmodernism as something that has made an impact on all areas of life and culture and can be construed as a "free-for-all"—indefinable and resisting definition. Nevertheless, they attempt a synthesis, stating it is a "loose umbrella term under whose broad cover can be encompassed at one and the same time a condition, a set of practices, a cultural discourse, an attitude and a mode of analysis." (ibid. 1994)

Lyotard postulates that postmodernism is essentially an extension of modernism, that the "post" in "postmodernism has the sense of a simple succession, a diachronic sequence of periods..." (in Docherty, 1993) and in which, despite this succession, there is still a possibility of being able to distinguish between the modern and the postmodern.

Featherstone (1991) in Usher and Edwards (1994) concurs with this last point Lyotard has made, but also argues that there has occurred "an epochal shift or break from modernity involving the emergence of a new social totality with its own distinct organising principles."

De Alba et al. (2000) cites Lyotard's definition of postmodern as

> the progressive emancipation of reason and freedom,
> the progressive or catastrophic emancipation of labor ...
> the enrichment of all through the progress of capitalist
> techno science, and even ... the salvation of creatures
> through the conversion of souls to the Christian
> narrative of martyred love.

She then notes that a "grand narrative" such as the Christian narrative "are the stories that cultures tell themselves about their own practices and beliefs in order to legitimate them. They function as a unified single story that purports to legitimate or found a set of practices, a cultural self-image, discourse, or institution" (ibid. 2000).

It is interesting to note that she applies this notion to the word "institution," which presumably includes academic institutions, which would, in turn, be encompassed in the ethos or paradigm (see Chapter

12) within which that institution operates. The type of environment an institution has is therefore dependent on the "grand narrative" in which it is expressed. Current institutions of education, as we have seen, are modernist constructions developed at the height of modernism to conform closely to the modernist way of thinking.

If we are in a new age of social discourse, however, then is it appropriate for us to continue to impose a modernist approach (current curricular structures) on those who will live and work in a postmodernist environment? Will public education's rooting in modernist discourse eventually result in its downfall? Perhaps most importantly, are we doing a service in providing what may be an outmoded social practice? Are we as educators in the process of alienating ourselves as a positive force for social construction and attitudes?

Mass public education may have difficulty with this postmodern lack of conformity. We find that students who are daily immersed in a postmodernist environment outside the classroom, but who then find themselves in a modernist classroom end up questioning (perhaps subconsciously) the outdated motivations for their education. In the end, those that realize the need to treat their educational experience as a "process of acquisition" will be the ones labeled as successful. But is this type of learning environment providing the best service for today's society?

Before proceeding further, it may be necessary to address the argument that postmodernism is only a product of western society and therefore does not count for the whole world. That may indeed be the case, but this post-modernist thinking is being slowly conveyed to all corners of the world through the process of globalization and technological innovation. Some cultures or nations are adept at stemming this postmodernist tide. However, the cultural flows outlined by Appadurai (1983) in Chapter 6 carry the necessary seed to introduce a postmodernist conception within these cultures and nations which have as yet been untouched. We can even argue that these same cultural flows generate a postmodernist state of mind—a perhaps necessary reaction to these flows which have been unleashed on the collective conscious. In every case, these cultural flows are powerful enough to affect some fundamental change within all cultures of the world. The potential does exist that cultural flows would completely nullify any ideological obstacles that have been erected to prevent such an intrusion—it is only a question of time before that happens. With this in mind, we can proceed with the view that postmodernism, while a product of particular western industrialized societies, will inevitably make its presence felt throughout the world, if it has not done so already.

We therefore need to integrate our contemporary social setting into our academic institutions, and this will necessarily have direct implications on the curriculum of an academic environment. As will be demonstrated later in the book (see Chapter 13), it is the curriculum that determines the type of learning environment the student will experience. The decision about the type of curriculum to be implemented, however, still rests with the educators themselves, implying that the necessary decision-making is a combination of internal (within the academic environment) and external (social) influence, and informed decisions about the most appropriate balance must be established. The link between the curriculum and postmodernism now becomes obvious. If education is to maintain its relevancy through this proper balancing of internal and external influence, then it cannot ignore the sociopolitical landscape it inhabits which, as stated previously, lies within a postmodernist environment.

Integrating a postmodernist environment into the academic structure, however, does not imply a free-for-all in the classroom where graffiti should be allowed on the walls and techno music pumped into the hallway. Nor does it imply a return to a 1970s approach of allowing students to create their own education through a series of electives and enforced self-determination (an ambitious and valiant attempt to address postmodernist educational issues). These ideas are indeed of the right orientation, but they provide no philosophical or practical guidance for the student to cope with the intricacies of today's social environment—an aspect which would have previously come from the "narrative" within the institution. Some may argue that even the idea of any philosophical guidance with its implications of a narrative of any sort runs contrary to the basis of postmodernity. In effect, mass education as it stands now is a system which still requires the cloak of modernity to function (for lack of a capable alternative) despite its presence in a postmodernist environment. Postmodernism can itself be construed as a "grand narrative" similar to existing systemic narratives found in education. In other words, this narrative is defined by its own imperatives.

In addition, the educational concepts listed above are only scratching the surface of a social paradigm that is extraordinarily complex in origin. We can, however, conclude that we need to attempt to develop a curriculum which is international in nature, which embraces a postmodernist perspective, and which aligns to the issues and philosophical orientations of today's society. Developing a structure such as this means perhaps letting go of "traditional" modern curricular conceptions (e.g. subject areas, current binary opposition expectations— please see glossary) and utilizing the "narrative" of contemporary culture to cover particular areas of concern for that society (see Chapter 4).

The term international, as has already been noted, may pose the most appropriate signifier for the educational environment. The focus within this context lies in the direction of allowing diversity in the classroom (ethnic, social, cultural). The concept of an international curriculum would therefore serve as a guiding force in the academic learning environment. In essence, it is an all-encompassing application of identifiable postmodernist norms which allow for "contemporary" intellectual growth. It is not meant to be prescriptive in nature—indeed the very idea of creating a prescriptive curricular structure is in itself a modernist conception. Instead, this postmodern curricular environment would best be served with a description of factors that conform to the "narrative" adopted for the student's education, interaction, and well–being. In other words, this "curriculum" application would not be limited to any specific educational structure; instead, it would be founded on the motivation to create a critically-minded, internationally focused, postmodernist perspective as the desired outcome in the student.

The concept of a postmodernist international curricular structure must therefore feature a focus on the commonality found within humanity. It must be accessible and committed to the individual, and it must be applicable, regardless of the geographical, cultural, or individual nature of the person. It must also be nonelitist in nature, meaning that it should be available to everyone regardless of social status or affiliation.

To have it otherwise would destroy the very essence and philosophical bearing of the entire scheme. The choice for the parent should not be:

Which cultural distinction would benefit my child the most?, but rather: Which educational environment would benefit my child so that he or she is able to become independent in an environment of globalization, technological saturation, and a waning of cultural differences?

In essence, it is imperative that if educators feel that the worst thing that could happen to a child's education would be to rely on the Internet (a physical manifestation of the postmodernist, globalizing world), then some guidelines should be developed to control this environment within which the child is already living and learning. Control does not mean that the teacher should make judgments that restrict or enforce information, but rather, the teacher should act as the "server" (in the Internet sense)—one who advertises and provides the information appropriate for an educational undertaking. The role of teacher would be to provide the human interaction required to guide the learner's choices in selecting the most beneficial and supportive information that's pertinent to that learner's life. This is not to imply, however, that all information will be supplied via the Internet, although the time may come when this may indeed be the case.

Perhaps the reason for the Internet's immense popularity is due to society subconsciously acknowledging that the modernist concept of organization no longer seems relevant to our "freedom-loving" postmodernist environment. To push the Internet metaphor further, the aim of developing a curricular structure that has universal features is similar to the development of the codes (e.g., Java Script) that provide universal access to the Internet. Regardless of the type of information (or subject) that a user wishes to download, this information adheres to a strict computer code in order for it to be universally accessible. Similarly, utilizing a curriculum that has as its underpinnings something that is universal in nature (the code), will guarantee the accessibility and user-friendliness of the information provided. In an educational sense, therefore, the code, or curriculum, is not a restrictor or enforcer of certain information types, but rather, it is the facilitator to a larger field of information.

Interestingly, de Alba et al. (2000) utilizes a similar metaphorical approach when addressing the changes that an effective curriculum would require within this postmodernist context.

We find curriculum still being construed very much in terms of "packages" of skills and content at a time when a metaphor like "platforms" seems much more apposite... In "techspeak" a platform refers to an undergirding operating logic or operating system upon which diverse, more immediate computing applications are based... The learner who masters "platforms" can proactively generate interpretations and frame designs that in turn generate their own learning and innovation agendas, and, ultimately, worldviews.... "Off the shelf" and "one size fits all" approaches to curriculum policy and design, although they have some scope for flexibility, subvert the understanding of the underlying principles of skills "platforms." The problem is that if teachers are to become oriented toward platform logic and away from packages, they need to understand and grasp the characteristically postmodern structure of knowledge (ibid. 2000).

This "postmodern structure of knowledge' means that the role of the educator within the school will have to change; no longer will they be the dispensers of knowledge, but as suggested, they will serve as "guides" in negotiating the *jungle* of information that is apparently at everyone's fingertips. Their main task in working with the student will be to develop the social survival techniques and critical thinking skills that students will need to live and work in an otherwise chaotic environment. As de Alba states, the teacher must master and then teach to the students the "platform" of necessary interpersonal and academic skills. Since the dawn of humanity, individuals have had to rely on each other to learn both academic and social skills, and we hope this aspect won't change. Unfortunately, however, if education does not find some way to address the postmodernist social discourse that presently pervades society, then conjectures on the outcome are all too easy. The Internet and its derivatives, already a prime source of information, will (if it hasn't already) easily and successfully compete against the schools' curriculum focus.

In many cases, we have yet to learn that restriction or enforcement (the word prohibition may bring historical frames of reference to mind) regarding access to information do not serve as a deterrent; they simply spark curiosity and rebelliousness in the individual. Individuals who are clever enough will eventually find a way to obtain the information (or product) nevertheless. In the past, the academic institution has managed to claim superiority in the dissemination of information and knowledge it considers to be important. A mentality that information is for those with privilege (e.g. academic, financial) was also prevalent. Both these stances are fast losing their potency. Instead it is becoming necessary to embrace the notion that information is now a free market commodity, and its dissemination is just a click or button away.

The educator, however, must still maintain a certain semblance to an informed chaperone. This position will be informed and characterized by a philosophical awareness and mindset that is extensively shared throughout the school community. Common characteristics which have received credibility as being universally applicable, and which would serve well as underlying criteria for such awareness could possibly include judicious use of a merit system to stimulate motivation, positive interaction and encouragement between student and educator, and a knowledge base that demonstrates not only depth in the subject being taught but also breadth in the relationships of that subject to other subjects and to the outside world.

It is possible that a postmodernist may frown on the notion of structure and label the whole idea as confused modernism. In fact, certain modernist traits are still necessary for continuity of purpose, as we have seen above and in Chapter 8 concerning the use of modernist notions by sovereign nations. If we accept the ideas of Lyotard, who treats postmodernism simply as an extension of modernism, it does not upset the postmodernist perspective. In every case, to attempt a complete reinvention of formal education may serve very little purpose, and indeed certain aspects of education (e.g. the physical plant, library media center, organization of teachers' salaries) are still a great aid to continuity and progress. The difference in concept from a postmodernist perspective lies in the abstraction of the goal or aim. No longer does the concept of the child-as-raw-material-to-create-the-finished-product apply. Instead perhaps the pre-Enlightenment concept of a master/apprentice relationship may be more rewarding as a source of future interaction. This is already evident in home-schooling structures.

In summary, achieving an awareness of an educational paradigm that can produce a more encompassing postmodernist perspective would benefit academic circles regardless of the level being scrutinized. The how, why, and what of academic traditions, exposed and hidden, need to be given closer scrutiny to determine their relevance to current social needs, and this can only be done with a desire to produce an educational environment relevant to the needs of today. Whose responsibility is it to scrutinize? As we shall see, the scrutiny rests with those who are best adept at affecting any important changes needed to the system. In effect, it is everyone who has a vested interest in building a capacity for public education for the Twenty-First century.

POSTMODERNISM AND EDUCATION IN A PUBLIC CONTEXT

Although this section of the chapter is brief in nature, in effect it is probably the most important. This brevity comes not from a lack of information about postmodernism, but rather from too much. Postmodernism after all, in its purest state, can be anything to anybody for any purpose deemed necessary or desired at the same time. Postmodernism can with very little effort change the modernist institution of public education so radically that we may not recognize the face of public education even over the course of our own lifetime

The question which may be asked at this point is: Are there are any existing models of institutional interaction which may serve as guidance for public education? In point of fact, it is likely that schools which serve the international community are already well positioned to create and develop a postmodernist academic environment, simply because of the type of environment in which they have chosen to exist.

To provide an example, an "international" school overseas often incorporates a plurality of cultures (as is the case in national systems). These schools make an effort to recognize their cultural plurality through fairs, parades, and events, and they often show a proactive awareness to the ills of the world (e.g., conducting research to understand the scope and magnitude of a specified problem, designing projects to come up with hypothetical solutions, participating in discussion circles on subjects such as rain forest conservation, drug use and abuse, etc.).

These efforts, though well-meaning, may only prove superficial in some situations, simply because the focus of the learning experience is lost behind the glitz and glamour of special events. This is not to detract from Hayden and Thompson's proposal (1998) of the importance of the **interstitial curriculum** as providing the curricular mortar for binding the curricular areas of interaction together, a concept which is echoed by Mackenzie in Hayden and Thompson (2000). The latter suggests that what is caught or experienced in an educational environment is just as important as what is taught. What these authors suggest is that it is necessary to know evaluate the core or "bricks" of the propagated curriculum. As was mentioned previously, is it patriarchal, "white" and western-centric, or is it something that addresses the needs of a clientele who will live in a highly pluralistic society? In other words, what color are the bricks? As Coulby and Jones (1995) point out, "School and university knowledge are vital elements in the reproduction of ethnocentrism. It is possible that they could be just as powerful elements in its reversal and ultimate elimination." With this in mind, we must inspect yet another philosophical facet relevant to our discussion—that of the political nature of the academic environment.

DISCUSSION AND REVIEW QUESTIONS FOR CHAPTER 9

1. What are the six basic assumptions for structuralism? How would you define structuralism?

2. Using the model of Gibson's Method of Structural Analysis, create a real-time model using an example from your school environment (e.g., you may draw from class activities you have done or you may also discuss relevant staff activities in a meeting).

3. Write a definition for modernism.

4. Write a definition for postmodernism.

5. Which definition was harder to compose and why?

6. Create a presentation on the Enlightenment Project detailing its influence, not only on society's thinking, but also through extrapolation on current educational ideologies.

7. Discuss the issues surrounding public education as a modernist structure in a postmodernist environment. What is in need of change for a more appropriate systemic structure?

8. In order to ensure relevancy to today's society and continuity in public education, explain what features you believe are necessary for developing an appropriate curricular program.

CHAPTER 10

THE POLITICS OF EDUCATION

A considerable amount of intellectual perspiration has dripped from the foreheads of educators in their attempt to determine the best curricular structure for the student. Questions such as what material they should teach, how much time they should allot to each subject, and what is the most effective way to deliver the espoused curriculum have attracted a substantial slice of educational attention; but what of the political nature of the curriculum?

Briefly, when we refer to the political nature of the curriculum, we concern ourselves primarily with those decision making processes which affect the outcome of the educational experience. This can happen on different levels of interaction as will be demonstrated in Figure 12.1 in Chapter 12.

Let us begin on a local level. Educators who are on the "front line" may find the concept of the curriculum being political to be burdensome and unnecessary. After all, what can possibly be political about "2+2," or that a water molecule is comprised of two hydrogen atoms and one oxygen atom? And yet, we are already faced with political decision-making aspects from these two simple examples. For example, at what age should these concepts be taught? Should concept attainment be accomplished through an exploratory, a Socratic, or a traditional (a politically sensitive word) methodology? In what language are we going to teach the material? Do we use computers to teach the concepts? Do we have the resources to buy computers? Perhaps more significantly for our purposes, how do we define our institution?

Governments, by their very nature, have often seen education as a source of political motivation. It is interesting to note that the majority of individuals in the world who were fortunate enough to attend high school probably attended a "government school," where the curriculum was inevitably approved by governmental authority. When governments make themselves responsible for education (an already political decision), it is always interesting to determine the motives behind their educational program. Prior examples can be seen from the forced language learning of Nazism and Communism to more present concerns, like having a properly educated workforce that will give the nation a competitive business, scientific, technological, or even ethical edge over other nations (Spring 1998).

Consequently, there appears to be strong reasons for national governments to develop their educational planning, starting from what is essentially a political arena. However, there may still be an unwillingness to acknowledge that politics exists in education, and this reluctance may stem perhaps from a further unwillingness to investigate the implications of such a connection. These perceptions and others, therefore, may have clouded the necessity for educators to contemplate the political focus of their occupation. This political focus is also clouded by the fact that it is now commonplace to face daily a saturation of information, techniques, methodologies, appraisal schemes and new materials which purport to supply teachers with all the right answers. But are these answers "right"? Have educators internalized the motivations and are they generally aware of what is being "fed" to the students from a political standpoint? Are educators aware of what they themselves are digesting?

Suppose, though, that we were to contemplate the idea of having a nonpolitical educational structure. If its political nature were to be exempted from the educational process, then it is very likely that many of the motivational incentives for the process would be lost. For example, there would be no need to agree on standards that gauge academic progress.

Things as simple as the daily routine of the school would be difficult to implement due to the lack of an administrative framework, which is the responsibility of the leadership. Perhaps there would be difficulty knowing what to teach, because the curricular motivation would no longer be linked to a particular mandate. In short, there would be very little recognizable structure, and this would transmit itself readily to all facets of the educational program, resulting in a complete lack of process—an aspect which current educational practice is loathe to do without.

De Alba (de Alba et al. 2000) also argues that the curriculum is a political-educational proposal constituted by a synthesis, or articulation, of cultural elements stemming from struggles, impositions, and negotiations among various social subjects (e.g., church, state, political parties, trade unions, community organizations, etc.) that sustain broad social-political projects and assume that society will be educated in accordance with such projects.

In his preface to the book *Pedagogy of the Oppressed* (Freire 1990), Shaull states:

> There is no such thing as a neutral educational process. Education either functions as an instrument which is used to facilitate the integration of the younger generation into the logic of the present system and bring about conformity to it, or it becomes "the practice of freedom," the means by which men and women deal critically and creatively with reality and discover how to participate in the transformation of their world.

It is worth noting that although Freire's book dealt primarily with teaching language to illiterates and the political factors that arise from this particular situation, the implications of writings are much more far-reaching. As Shaull once more aptly points out, our "advanced technological society is rapidly making objects of most of us and subtly programming us into conformity to the logic of its system. To the degree that this happens, we are also becoming submerged in a new 'culture of silence'" (Freire 1990).

In effect, Shaull is observing the perils of too much information, or as it has been termed, "information overload." There is also the danger of having human beings lose their identity due to the overpowering influences which ride on the coat tails of the technological revolution.

Appadurai (1988) addresses this submergence of personal identity, however, and replaces it with images and concepts which he portrays through the flows described previously. Shaull has only demonstrated the possible result from these cultural flows, and that is the development of a "culture of silence" brought on by an inability to understand daily experience. We can see evidence of this "culture of silence" in people's daily decision-making processes, when they make decisions that are based on readily accessible information, instead of relying on personal knowledge or experience. In every case, from a public education perspective, the implications may surpass even those already stated by Shaull—that public schools may also be suffering from this "culture of silence"—not because of an inability to read (as it was described in Freire's writings), but because of an inability to decipher the conflicting messages found within the school and its adjoining community. This situation creates a less-than-satisfactory philosophical and ideological understanding for the school and its curriculum. It translates into a "chaotic" stance, which is transferred to the student through various curricular and extracurricular channels, and which exacerbates an already complex situation. As a result, we develop our very own hybrid that mutates from a "culture of silence" to a "cultural silence."

De Alba et al. (2000) concurs with this analysis, stating:

> one of the most serious problems confronting us at present in the area of the curriculum is the lack of sociopolitical projects (or social direction) that would allow us to (re)constitute the curriculum-society link .... The various social subjects, the projects they represented, and the struggles among them were reasonably clear and understood and were recognized as legitimate bases for social organization and development ... (and) new hegemonic practices can be articulated. (Parenthetical comments mine)

There is therefore an apparent danger that the school environment will perpetuate the hegemonic perspective Freire is concerned about, and this, together with the loss of a curricular focus within the same context, as demonstrated by de Alba, could also lead to a **hegemonic paradigm** within the institution. The term hegemonic in this case refers to the situation where an environment is compromised to appease the dominant party and maintain the status quo.

This status quo can be perpetuated by decision-making processes that (intentionally as described by Freire, or unintentionally as mentioned by de Alba) promote a "cultural silence" within specific members of a given population segment. This cultural silence may be indicated through the situation where the rich and privileged remain unaware of their position, or they are taught to take their educational experience for granted. Perhaps more importantly, this cultural silence may take on the form where minority groups within an institution intentionally lose their particular cultural identity in an effort to avoid possible ostracism from the dominant group. It may be that these political inequalities are unknowingly built into the curriculum, which in turn lessens the chance for the institution to recognize and change, thus compromising efforts to promote a true international education within the institution's environment.

Traditional school situations have generally led to what Freire describes as "**banking education**":

> Education thus becomes an act of depositing, in which the students are the depositories and the teacher is the depositor. Instead of communicating, the teacher issues communiqués and makes deposits which the students patiently receive, memorize, and repeat (Freire 1990).

From an academic curricular perspective, this may be no longer the case, but what of the other aspects to the curriculum—chiefly the pastoral and hidden curricular structures? With these two curricular structures, the banking system may not be as direct, but it will still have an effect on the outcome of the learners by influencing the course of the formal curriculum. Within Freire's banking metaphor, one could consider the effect on the outcome as "interest" on the principal. If we as educators have been charged with preparing the student to enter society, then should we not also address those issues that are perplexing our students and the world at large?

To this end, a school should promote a transformative intellectual environment. The latter refers to the notion that the individual is given the opportunity to think critically, not only about the concept being presented, but also to have the ability to take the basic concept and transform it for positive implementation into the current social environment. An intellectual environment such as this would allow students to realize the full implications of the society they will enter, and more importantly, to enact change where they feel it is necessary. The school, however, must provide more than just token opportunities for the student to develop and evaluate constructive, re-creative powers. The school must also be aware that it needs to pay more than lip service to the ideological focus it promotes in its philosophical statements. Perhaps even most importantly, schools must take the time to ensure that the transformational concepts underpinning this ideological focus are present within the interaction of the school. Failure to develop these ideological concepts in just one part of the school community will most likely corrupt any headway made in other areas.

The outcome resulting from this paradigmatic shift in the basic fundamentals of the educational process could result in a more proactive stance that will empower all involved. A focus such as this will give a direction in which everyone is contributing to the positive development of the student, who will adopt these ideological qualities and use them far beyond the time spent in a primary or secondary educational environment. In an educational context where the focus would be on producing an "international awareness" in the student, it is imperative that students appreciate the fact that the decisions they will make in the future may have global implications. Even if they don't fully understand the scope of those decisions, we would still be amiss not to teach those values which are necessary for a student's successful integration into an international environment.

The academic (formal), pastoral, and hidden curricular structures mentioned previously play a vital role in transforming the sociocultural structure of the school, and a paradigm is created from the interaction within the school's environment. The culmination of this paradigm is the learner's tendency towards a certain type of intellectual focus. For this reason, it is necessary for an academic institution to have a firm grasp on all three of these curricular structures to affect any intellectual stance which the institution may purport to carry.

Therefore, when referring to public education, and regardless of its location, a school should be able to call itself an institution of "contemporary international education" by demonstrating its paradigmatic stance as falling on the left side of the intellectual spectrum as indicated in Fig. 10.1.

Transformative Intellectual	Critical Intellectual	Accommodating Intellectual	Hegemonic Intellectual
------------------------/------------------------------/------------------------------/----------------------------			
International perspective			Local perspective

Fig. 10.1 – *The intellectual spectrum and the educational perspective it perpetuates*

Because it places the local perspective with hegemonic intellectualism, and the international perspective with transformative intellectualism, one may find this particular spectrum too general. In fact, as we have already argued that there is a basic necessity in today's western society to look past the comfort of one's own "backyard" and to embrace the demands of the new and foreign. This, in turn, implies that an intellectual stance of a transformative nature would aid in creating and developing an international perspective. Maintaining a protective and inward-looking stance, however, may only perpetuate any existing hegemonic tendencies, which may, in turn, be counterproductive for all levels of our society.

Additionally, the concepts of local and international outlined above are not based on physical or geographical boundaries but on intellectual and abstract boundaries which human beings create for themselves. In today's world, however, borders that are both physical and mental may no longer be fully serving their purpose. In fact, they may be acting as an impediment for a society that is attempting to explore and understand beyond such artificial boundaries. The time has passed when we could safely assume that all we need to worry about is our own backyard. As a society, we are confronted daily with problems and opportunities that stem from the entire world, and to ignore these aspects only enforces a "culture of silence." The world, through technology and invention, has indeed become a very small place, and this trend can only increase. If we as educators do not take the time to prepare the student properly, then we are not fulfilling the obligation which we have made our vocation.

The appropriate paradigm of an international school should therefore be enabling students to integrate into the appropriate community by realizing their ability to create positive, transformative contributions that have the potential to affect the global environment. In fact, an international school can call itself an international school only if it has achieved a paradigmatic stance that is based on its political convictions—convictions that are demonstrated through curricula that produce transformative intellectual individuals.

DISCUSSION AND REVIEW QUESTIONS FOR CHAPTER 10

1. Discuss to what degree education is politicized. Is there any area within education that does not have a political aspect? Why?

2. What are the influences on education that contributes to its political environment?

3. Discuss Shaull's statement that we are all suffering from information overload leading to a culture of silence. How do you perceive this information overload as affecting the individual, the community, the region, etc.?

4. What is different between a culture of silence and a cultural silence? What implications do each hold for education?

5. What are the three standard types of curriculum found in an academic environment?

6. Why is it important to keep these curricula in mind when determining a school environment?

Chapter 11

The Concept of Culture in Education

We may surmise that different sociocultural influences affect the political nature of an educational setting. This notion of cultural input is particularly relevant in light of the growing influx of different cultures and ideologies in today's public education system, creating an environment that is at times ill suited and even hostile to different outside influences.

While in the past, the relative homogeneity of the clientele made it easy to create a definable education system, that this is no longer the case. Several systemic issues can and do arise within the educational environment, including the potential of a curricular process being determined almost exclusively by the dominant culture within that community, to the exclusion of perhaps other minority parties. There is also the unprecedented fact that outside influences, such as the current wave of technology (not to mention gangs and their entrapments), have infringed substantially on the traditional learning environment. These factors force educators to make adjustments to their approaches and methodologies so that they can maintain their effectiveness and relevancy as educators.

In this chapter we will explore the sociocultural impact of contemporary society on education. It is the author's belief that if educators can understand the cultural implications of their learning community, then it will become easier for them to devise applicable strategies of educational development for the community in which they are working.

There are already several models that explain the phenomenon of cultural influence. One particularly interesting approach is the analogy of the iceberg (Fennes and Hapgood 1997). As in the actual physical iceberg, only a small portion is visible above the surface. In cultural terms, that which is visible may include the arts, cooking, clothing, and those things that are easily experienced through everyday interaction.

Under the surface, however, lies a plethora of cultural biases, which may perhaps be determined from the visible parts, but in all likelihood are more clearly understood through a series of complex relationships to the visible parts. These cultural biases are likely to remain out of everyday awareness. Levi-Strauss was concerned with determining the underpart of this cultural iceberg through his use of structuralist methodology and his concept of binary oppositions (see Chapter 9). These *binary oppositions* were also the impetus for *transformations* that occurred within a specific cultural context (Lane, 1970). These transformations are in essence changes in the relationship between the two objects or bodies of concern, reached perhaps through compromise or the laws of the society.

Another interesting aspect that may be helpful in determining the importance of culture in the political landscape of the school is defined by Hofstede and Bond (1988), who suggest that culture is mental programming. In this particular instance, the authors refer to the notion that patterns of thinking, feeling, and potential acting are learned through a lifetime as mental programs. They further make the point that since such programming is at least partly shared with people who live or lived within the same environment, then culture is a collective phenomenon.

There are three levels of mental programming; the first level is human nature (the operating system), which is specific to a certain group or category; the second level is learned culture, which is specific to a certain group or category; and the third level is the personality of the individual.

Although the above treatment can be construed as somewhat abbreviated, it is enough that one can now begin to see some interesting notions coming to light. In the case of a public school, for instance, a number of binary oppositions appear which need to be resolved on a daily basis through existing structures or ideals. This in effect produces a microculture. As Hofstede and Bond (ibid.) point out, however, there are still a number of cultural conditions which directly influence this microculture in the institution we have labeled a public school. The complexity of the public school is largely a result of its abundant cultural and social influences, all of which effect the school's sociopolitical environment. The resultant difficulties must be solved to maintain a smoothly operating setting, however, and through this process, there is always the danger that the school's political orientation can become dominated by the most powerful group in the microculture.

At this point, diversity becomes particularly important. The most powerful group can now decide which action to take. In essence, this group has the opportunity to implement the type of educational outcome which adheres to the political focus it has embraced, and this focus is decided by the additive experiences of the dominant group on all three levels of programming as described above. The main question for the dominant group to decide is, should it promote a perspective that is hegemonic in character, or should it promote a perspective that is transformative in character? In the case of a public school, a transformative focus would facilitate the concept of *intercultural learning* (Fennes and Hapgood 1997), which is perhaps a more beneficial road for education to take.

To proceed further, there are two principles that we must keep in mind for intercultural learning to take place. The first is cultural relativism (Gollnick and Chin 1998), which means that there is no hierarchy of culture. The second is the principle of reciprocity (Gollnick and Chin 1998), which implies that intercultural learning is not a one-way process; neither does it aim at assimilation, but rather, its goal is sharing equal status, interdependence, responsibility, and cooperation—all of which are transformative notions.

The very nature of a school, therefore, means that the decisions the school takes in all of its areas, be it curriculum-writing or the type of food served in the cafeteria, lead to an underlying understanding of the school environment. The question is, can we maintain sufficient control over the cultural environment to create a multicultural learning

DISCUSSION AND REVIEW QUESTIONS FOR CHAPTER 11

1. Discuss the issues and possible political orientations of a school culture that is dominated by the most powerful group. What are the implications for individuals who are in a leadership setting?

2. Explain how the two principles of intercultural learning can impact a public school environment. What other factors could promote an effective intercultural learning environment?

CHAPTER 12

DEFINING THE CONCEPT OF "CURRICULUM"

This chapter attempts to shed light on the way we currently use notions of curriculum, their structure, and their implications for future curricular orientation. Some of the concepts within this chapter are ideological and philosophical innovations that may provide insight into areas hitherto not explained completely in public education. It sets the stage for a discussion about how the curriculum acts as a vehicle to shepherd public education into particular organizational domains. It also describes how those same domains are based on a historically referenced paradigm that may not be able to fully service the needs of contemporary learners. In other words, the educational curricula are the frameworks by which we can facilitate the learning and understanding of contemporary social dialectics to best prepare the student for tomorrow's world.

CHARACTERISTICS OF A CURRICULUM

In attempting to define the characteristics of a curriculum, Marsh (1992) focuses on issues surrounding the subject matter to be taught, such as the number and type of subjects. In fact, Marsh has cited that this subject diversity has forced education to think within *curriculum frameworks* that he defines as "a group of related subjects which fit together according to a predetermined set of criteria..." Marsh continues by citing another definition for curricular framework from Kerr (1989) as "guides that have been explicitly designed and written to assist school communities of teachers, students, and parents in their curriculum decision making." Kerr is also cited in another book (Lawton, 1978) where he defines the curriculum as "all the learning which is planned and guided by the school, whether it is carried out in groups or individually, inside or outside the school"(Kerr 1968).

Lewy demonstrates that the concept of curriculum can take many varied forms, with there being as many different curricular concepts as there are individuals who conceive them. He then proceeds to list nine definitions to support his statement (Lewy 1991). One seemingly important aspect to his argument is that "it is necessary to study different and many more things when 'curriculum' is defined as 'all the experiences one has under the jurisdiction of a school,' which is more appropriate as a definition for a curricular structure rather than 'as a course of study.'" (Emphasis mine.)

Hass and Parkay (1993) provide the following definition of curriculum:

> all the experiences that individual learners have in a program education whose purpose is to achieve broad goals and related specific objectives, which is planned in terms of a framework of theory and research or past and present professional practice.

These definitions point to an extremely interesting perception of curriculum—that it is more than just the content of the material being taught. In fact, the curriculum appears to weave itself through several areas of the educational environment. It might be said, therefore, that the structure of a curriculum is dependent on the elements which surround it. At the same time, all parties in the educational environment (see the SPACE factor in Chapter 4) are directly affected by the curriculum that is implemented, and this in turn means a paradigm has been created. Further investigation into this particular view of a curriculum, however, requires additional clarification before we can proceed toward a working definition that is suitable for our purposes.

Peter J. Zsebik, Ph.D.

CURRICULAR STRUCTURES WITHIN A CURRICULUM

The one aspect a teacher in any educational context constantly confronts is determining the nature of the information and skills to be taught in an academic context; that is, the academic or formal curricular structure. Many teachers are aware of the parameters of this "academic" structure, having been involved in its construction at one point or another in their career. It is essentially what may be termed as the nuts and bolts that allow the teacher to effectively function in the classroom. It is the element that creates a unity of purpose and a map to negotiate the educational interaction. These aspects are the curricular structure.

As a note, if the condition of education is to be transformative, then it is necessary that the teacher be allowed some autonomy within the working environment. As teachers, we are given responsibility not only to teach that which has been mandated, but to also provide opportunities for the learner to use this information in ways that guarantee a successful and transformative learning outcome. It follows then that a teacher must have some intellectual control over the program for which he or she is responsible. Without this intellectual control, the teacher's effectiveness as an agent of education is greatly diminished.

If this statement is accepted as true for the academic curricular structure, however, then there is still the following further implication: how far does the teacher's responsibility for intellectual control extend? Is it limited only to the academic program or does it extend further into the general ethos of the school? Or if we take this further, is the school and its curriculum responsible for providing a context that is strictly for academic growth, or does it also have the responsibility of creating a complete learning environment? Exactly how much responsibility must an educator assume? And in what way are those responsibilities to be carried out? While the answers to these questions may strike one as absurdly easy to negotiate, further clarification regarding the extent of this responsibility becomes much more difficult.

THE IMPACT OF THE ACADEMIC, PASTORAL, AND HIDDEN CURRICULAR STRUCTURES

Much research has been done to attempt to clarify those particular elements within school curricula that are, inadvertently or otherwise, being taught. While a number of variables do exist within the context of these curricular elements, the curriculum of a school has generally been considered to have three major divisions or structural elements as outlined by Lawton (1978).

> *The Academic Curriculum*—"What might traditionally considered to be the curriculum e.g., 'subjects' taught in school."

> *The Pastoral Curriculum*—"To include personal guidance (e.g., social skills, relationships), educational guidance (e.g., study and information-finding skills) and vocational guidance (e.g., learning about careers and occupations)."

> *The Hidden Curriculum*—might be defined as adaptive learning "unespoused and unacknowledged by the school: the 'hidden messages' students receive as part of their schooling."

Even after identifying these particular aspects of the curriculum, however, much of what goes on within an academic institution is left very much to chance. This chance is often caused by an unbalanced lack of clarity and goal identification occurring within the three types of curricula listed above. And yet, to some extent, an ethos, as identified by Matthews (1988) and others, still exists in these same academic institutions, and this ethos may provide a basis for a cohesive curriculum where all three curricular areas (as listed above) are connected to the same outcome.

Let us look at another element that gives an indication of this notion. Oftentimes administrators who are required to hire new personnel rely very much on their intuition and a minimum of information as they attempt to determine whether an individual will fit into their school. It is equally hard for the teacher in this same situation to know if this is the environment in which he or she would like to teach. Even if the intuitive process is correct from both sides, there is still a period of adaptation before a teacher feels comfortable (see Chapters 7 and 8 to review transformational concepts). In other words, there is an episode of learning (whether this is conscious or subconscious) before the teacher gains a certain amount of control and confidence over the various curricular structures.

Problems may arise, however, when the treatment given to the academic curriculum falters for the other curricular structures. This extends especially into the Pastoral and Hidden curricular structures, where much more is taken for granted all elements in the school setting (see SPACE chapter 4). Interestingly, the Pastoral Curriculum area has not been completely ignored. In the early part of this century, a national curriculum in the United Kingdom initiated a program entitled PSHE (Personal, Social, Health Education), which is based on an ethos and values statement outlining twelve ethos indicators. Within this framework, one can find a structure that attempts to identify the pastoral needs of the student, and these needs are determined by the student's academic year. From this example, we can see a desire to address issues of the ethos of the school, and that it plays an important part in the delivery of this particular structure. While some have admitted that it is necessary to overlap the pastoral and the academic curricula (Marland 1980), the reality of the practice is often at odds with the theory in U.K. schools (Drake in Hayden and Thompson, eds. 1998); as a result, this aspect is still left largely to chance.

This is particularly relevant for public education in any context. From a psychological standpoint, lack of a formal structure often leads to a haphazard application of the educational product. This haphazardness is not really the fault of the teacher, who is trying his or her best to demonstrate what he or she personally believes to be the necessary Pastoral curricular model. There is also a greater likelihood that if teachers do not come from the same cultural or educational background, then certain distinct cultural elements from the teacher, perhaps an emphasis on certain festive occasions to the exclusion of others, or dismissal of a student's previous native experiences, will be applied or transferred unwittingly. Actions such as these (intentional or unintentional) leave the student with very little else but conflicting messages due to the exposure to different teachers' sets of criteria. At this point, the lack of guidance for the Hidden Curriculum enters into the discussion.

The majority of schools do attempt to address this seeming inadequacy through their "school philosophy," but the danger is that this school philosophy, which has been so carefully worded to achieve a "proper" balance of idealism and practicality, is paid its due only on infrequent occasions. In private education settings, it may be regarded only as a hurdle for accreditation, or possibly even as a political battlefield in which everyone involved must exercise their right to be included. In public education settings, the idea of a hidden curriculum is relegated to the school's overall reputation. The school philosophy therefore may be consigned to the position of becoming only a description of the general character of the school. Equally, it may achieve simply an idealistic description of what the school hopes to deliver. It may also pose as a missed opportunity to guide the interaction between the sociopolitical influences within the school and their participation within its environment.

All aspects of the school community, as outlined in the SPACE Factor (see Chapter 4), may carry an abundance of varying cultural and political inputs. The resulting mélange generates an environment of blurred values and "unguided" determinism, especially if the administration, the curriculum, and the educator are working at cross-purposes. Worse, the school may possess little academic purpose because it lacks an agreed institutional philosophical grounding, particularly if the latter stretches no further than providing generalizations in the school's statement of philosophy.

From this vantage, it becomes relatively easy to see the appropriateness of having some sort of a structure in place that would address these issues. In other words, some academic guideline that would help to define the otherwise seemingly muddled area of a school's overall educational output would need to be put forward. The problem, however, is where to begin.

Peter J. Zsebik, Ph.D.

DEFINING THE PARADIGMATIC CURRICULUM

The concept of an international school that possesses its own unique philosophical perspective should not be disregarded entirely simply because it cannot be defined. If, as we have seen, there are several separate and distinct parts to the school (the SPACE Factor) together with the different types of curricula (which fall under the C in SPACE), each of which contributes in its own way to the creation of a particular environment (or paradigm), then we may assume that a cohesiveness—or ethos—for that institution has been created. This author has determined that this paradigm primarily the result of the elements in SPACE on the output of the institution. This paradigm can be evidenced by the resultant outcomes (student success) of the specified school, and this paradigm further can be defined through the curricular programs (academic, pastoral, hidden) that provide guidance to all the other curricular elements found in the institution. The function of the "paradigmatic curriculum," therefore, would be to describe the sociopolitical environment necessary to achieve the appropriate outcome, which in this case, is an "internationally minded public education."

This paradigmatic curriculum, therefore, is defined by the social paradigm in which a society finds itself. The paradigm for mass education in western society began as modernist, and now it is post-modernist. Slattery (1995) states that a "post-modern worldview allows educators a way out of the turmoil of contemporary schooling ... (and) postmodernism offers the best theoretical paradigm for exploring curriculum development." In effect this means that this paradigmatic curriculum, which was once modern in its orientation, must now begin to shift into a more postmodern stance.

Slattery has identified at least eleven different perspectives of postmodernism, but the ones that are more pertinent to education include: an emerging historical period that transcends the modern industrial and technological age; a philosophical movement that seeks to expose the internal contradictions of metanarratives by deconstructing modern notions of truth, language, knowledge, and power; a radical eclecticism (not compromise and consensus); and finally, an acknowledgement and celebration of otherness, particularly from racial and gendered perspectives (Slattery, 1995). It may be that this last one could be the key to the growing success of the twenty-first-century public school, in which case this researcher believes it should be, but does this also mean that a dichotomy exists between the perceived function versus the expected function of the public school within the postmodernist environment?

If this paradigmatic structure were formalized, it would provide the foundation for the school's philosophical focus, and it would outline the basic principles which would determine the type of sociopolitical outcome educators would want to inculcate into their charges. This would in turn define the outcomes of the other three curricula mentioned previously. A visual representation of the overall curricular structure might look somewhat like a pizza, as demonstrated in the diagrams below.

It is important to note that the paradigmatic curriculum is completely separate and distinct from the other curricula. The difference lies in the premise that the paradigmatic curriculum would serve as a general guide, an overview, or in this case a foundation which supplies an ideological footing for teaching academic and curricular concepts, thereby governing them and giving these three curricula a common focus from which to draw. In effect, the paradigmatic curriculum would be the driving agent for the creation of a complete curricular picture within any educational context. It would usurp the mission statement or school philosophy as the motivating force behind the school's raison d'être, with the added advantage of having the paradigmatic curriculum be completely integrated into the life of the school through the other three curricular areas. The paradigm (or ethos) of the institution is defined. As a hierarchical notion, we might envision the following:

Mission statement →Philosophy→ Paradigm

While this schemata does little more than allow a brief intellectual summary of the process which would create a paradigm, it is important to note that a more concrete form would also need to be created. The Scottish Education Authority's PSHE document cited above could provide some insight as to the form of such a document. A document such as this, together with extended training sessions appropriate to each of the individuals found within the SPACE Factor, would contribute greatly to the awareness of each necessary aspect as it relates to the ethos of the institution.

To continue, Figure 12.1 supplies us well with a visual representation of the function of the Paradigmatic Curriculum; it serves as a base from which the other curricula can find functional stability. Additionally, however, if one were to continue with the metaphor of the pizza, it would not be until you have put all the ingredients (SPACE Factor, Academic, Hidden, Pastoral curricula) together and put it into the oven that you would end with a pizza that truly describes the *paradigm* of a school.

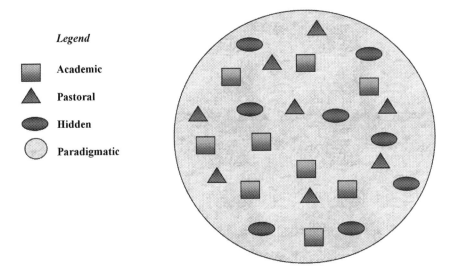

Fig. 12.1 - ***Overall Curricular Structure Addressing Paradigmatic Issues***

The final pizza will look something like the second diagram in Fig. 12.2. below.

One more aspect of the pizza needs to be addressed, however, and that is, metaphorically speaking, the quality of the curricular ingredients. This condition of quality has nothing to do with the freshness of the curricular structures, or the quantity of the material used to transmit it; rather, this quality concentrates precisely on the paradigmatic focus of the curriculum. It is this paradigmatic focus which is the major contributing factor to the type of paradigm the school has to offer.

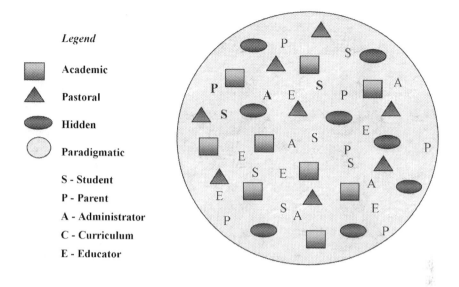

Legend

■ Academic

▲ Pastoral

⬭ Hidden

◯ Paradigmatic

S - Student
P - Parent
A - Administrator
C - Curriculum
E - Educator

Fig 12.2 – ***Visual Representation of the Paradimatic Plane in a public school***

THE PARADIGMATIC MODEL FOR CURRICULAR CONSTRUCTION

To create an effective and worthwhile definition of curriculum, we must take one last step that draws all the different aspects that have been mentioned into one cohesive picture—a visual construction that explains the general development of any curricular structure found in an academic environment. That structure is what this author calls the "Paradigmatic Model of Curricular Construction."

This model conceptualizes a curriculum that provides a philosophical foundation for the other three curricula within the academic environment: the academic, pastoral and hidden curricula (see Figure 12.1 above). This model is in effect an all-encompassing ideological description of the environmental structure of an institution, beginning with the elements of SPACE through to its distinctive ethos which, in turn, creates the paradigm within which the institution resides.

For the paradigm to become fully active, however, it must pass through a series of filters. These filters are determined by the infrastructure of the school community which in turn are created by the elements involved in creating the school community. To better clarify this infrastructure and the filtering process, a diagram has been developed (see Fig 12.3).

The top of this model is dominated by what has been termed the SPACE Factor (see Chapter 4). The SPACE Factor is essential as a beginning point because it defines the social structure of the institution. In addition, the SPACE Factor also defines who will be involved in producing the decisions which directly affect the various curricula, once the social structure has been determined. It is important to note that the curriculum (including hidden, pastoral, and academic) in SPACE (detailed as C) at this point is undefined.

While in practice, a curriculum that serves as the driving force may indeed exist at the outset, in reality, developing the actual curricula (and their inherent mutations) generally follows other structures, elements, and decisions (e.g., registering the students, hiring the staff, and preparing and maintaining the physical building). It is therefore necessary that we reallocate the curriculum further down the model. This author also maintains that the curriculum in practice is not the same as the curriculum chosen at the initial stages, regardless of the sociopolitical setting. In other words, even if the curricula have been scrutinized, labeled, and branded, there is still room to mutate and further define each curriculum based on the chosen environment and the other elements in the SPACE Factor.

To leave the curriculum entirely out of SPACE however, is unjustified because it is the curriculum which serves as the agent that brings together otherwise divergent individuals for a common purpose. In other words, as was already stated, no element of SPACE can be removed without serious jeopardy to the concept of a school community.

Once those individuals who share an interest in the development of the curricula have been selected, the creation of a sociopolitical landscape (the school community as it is defined through its population), or "schoolscape," is created. This step is essential in that it produces the overriding cultural flow (Appadurai 1994) which defines every sociological event that occurs within the school community. In effect, the paradigm of the institution has been defined.

Once this cultural flow is filtered within an academic structure, it is then transferred to the next step, which constitutes the crux of the entire process: creating the paradigmatic curriculum, which creates the paradigm of the specified school. In other words, the paradigmatic curriculum demonstrates the paradigm that has been created through the sociological interaction of the individuals who are concerned with developing a specific school community. This paradigm is what defines every curricular and extra-curricular decision and outcome. To put it briefly, the paradigm (or ethos) is the **gestalt**, or overall state of mind, which encompasses the sum total of all sociopolitical interaction within the specified site.

It is also at this point that academic priorities of a school community may diverge. The divergence can take many directions, but in general terms, it may be construed that the major divergences stemming from the Curricular Filter can be gauged against the political spectrum (see Chapter 10). These particular filters are comprised of sociopolitical characteristics which define the paradigmatic parameters to be incorporated into the general curricular structures in question, especially those surrounding the academic, pastoral, and hidden curricular structures. In other words, this filter constitutes guidelines which the school community adopts for the purpose of determining and creating its relevant curricular situation.

In this model, a divergence shows that the school implements a curricular filter that creates a curriculum with a *transformative* perspective. A divergence to the middle promotes a curriculum with an *accommodating* perspective. A divergence to the other side of the model leads to a curriculum with a *hegemonic* perspective. At this point, the paradigm of the learning outcome established through the Curriculum in the SPACE Factor has been defined, and a school community with a clear focus has been established.

It now becomes clear that perhaps one of the most important elements to assess when determining the academic situation of a school is the curriculum and the related curricular structures which the school has incorporated into its environment. It is therefore time to turn one's mind to defining the areas to research.

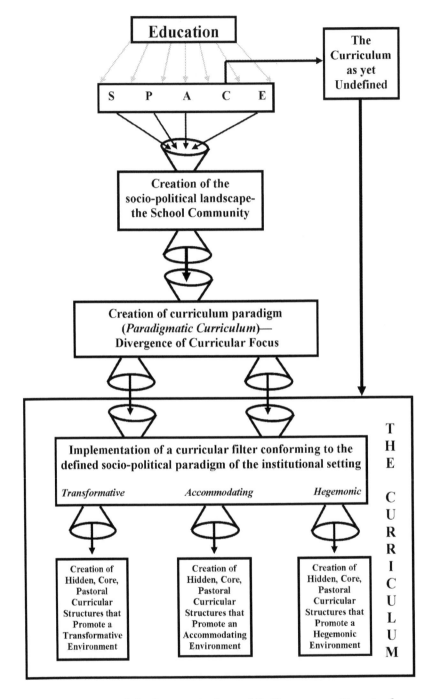

Fig 12.3 – *Model of Socio-Political Influence on Curricular Creation in Education*

DISCUSSION AND REVIEW QUESTIONS FOR CHAPTER 12

1. Create a three column table. Each column will be headed by the three types of curricula (Academic, Pastoral, Hidden). List under the appropriate curricular heading whether the activity you decide on is Academic, Pastoral, or Hidden in nature. Your parameters are defined by *one day's activities in your school.*

2. Discuss what conclusions you can come to regarding the type of curricular activity found in a typical school setting. Were there any surprises? Discuss.

3. Discuss and create a working definition for curriculum. Are there any similarities or differences between yours and the definitions that have been identified?

4. It is the teacher's responsibility to teach all the curricular structures (academic, pastoral, hidden) to create the school's paradigmatic curriculum. Do you agree or disagree? Share your answers.

5. What other issues in the school environment could hinder change at the curricular level? How would you overcome these obstacles?

6. What advantages are apparent in determining the sociopolitical paradigm of an institution? What are the challenges?

7. Explain the use of a paradigmatic curriculum. How is it beneficial to the cohesiveness of the institutional programme?

8. Outline the issues for public education surrounding the following quote from page 145, "*a dichotomy exists between*

> *the perceived function versus the expected function of the public school within the postmodernist environment."*

9. Discuss the importance of the curricular structures in defining a learning environment. What aspect of the curriculum would you consider the most important? Why?

10. Explain the notion of "schoolscape." What benefits can you see for consciously defining the schoolscape?

CHAPTER 13

AN OVERVIEW OF CURRICULAR MOTIVATION

To determine a future course of action within an academic context, educators have often searched for motivation which they could utilize to achieve a cohesive educational program. Invariably, they then translate what they agree upon into documentation to inform the educational process. This documentation answers the questions, "What information will we teach?" and "Why are we teaching this information to the student?" In effect, curricular programming is the sum total of all the external, noneducational forces that motivate the broad curricular priorities and the directions utilized.

These motivating influences provide the necessary stimulus for the players in SPACE (see Chapter 4) to achieve results considered necessary for a successful life in the world.

A HISTORY OF CURRICULAR MOTIVATION

Historically, education has turned to society to help determine what would be of most value to teach. As an example, we can turn to Parkay (1992) who relates the observations of curriculum historians Gwynn and Chase. These individuals suggested five factors that "influenced our schools' curricula at various points in our (American) history":

(1) religious sentiments (approx. 1620–1740)
(2) political factors (approx. 1770–1860)
(3) utilitarian aims (approx. 1860–1920)
(4) the push for mass education (approx. 1890–present)
(5) the push for excellence (approx. 1920–present)

The history of English education also exhibits the attribute of gauging society to help guide its curricular motivation. Lawton (1975) has neatly identified the different stages of English education up until the mid 1970s. The stages of English education as identified by Lawton are as follows:

- *Stage 1* (1920s and 30s): Pressure for access to secondary education
- *Stage 2* (1940s and 50s): Growth of secondary education for all in the diluted form of a tripartite system, with the gradual realization that it was unworkable and unjust.
- *Stage 3* (1960s): Growth of comprehensive schools— common secondary schools theoretically presenting equal educational opportunity or equally fair chances for all pupils but which were far from successful in practice.
- *Stage 4* (1970s): An increase in interest in questions about the secondary curriculum...What is the point of the secondary curriculum?

As a note, prior to the first stage cited above, a two-tier system within England and Wales was in place: "On the one hand there was the public school/grammar school tradition of education for leadership, which gave rise to a curriculum for 'Christian gentlemen' who would become the leaders of society...On the other hand the elementary school tradition was especially intended to train the 'lower orders'. Elementary schools were designed to produce a labour force able to understand simple written instructions and capable of making elementary calculations— skills necessary for a competent factory worker" (Lawton 1975).

Both of these national examples vividly portray the flowering of curricular motivation based on the "prevailing needs of the society and our views of children and how they learn ....The curriculum must, somehow, reflect the beliefs, values, and needs of widely different groups ..." (ibid.), or as cited in Chapter 12, it may also reflect the beliefs of the most dominant groups (politically and economically) in society. It is apparent within a national context that the motivational aspects of curricular creation are dependent on current trends in society. It is also interesting to note that the last two curricular motivators listed within the North American context have worked in conjunction with each other, and that in both national examples, changes in curricular motivation have undergone more and more frequent shifts in emphasis since the 1800s.

These more frequent shifts have resulted in a number of curricular structures that attempt to create more specific educational objectives, and the latter are formulated to suit the parties who have an interest in that particular educational outcome. In fact, it is difficult to really generate a historical perspective of curriculum without also having to generate a perspective on world history. Indeed, it can be justly said that education is not independent of the environment in which it is situated. As de Alba (2000) points out,

> these (curricular) stories have their own built-in ends or teleologies, which change according to who is telling the story, to whom, and for what political purpose. It appears however that there is agreement that highly significant social, technological, economic and political changes have occurred since the end of World War Two ... Moreover, they agree that this change in some way or other bespeaks a new sensibility and worldview: that these technological and sociopolitical transformations amount to a sea change. The terms "postmodernism" and "the postmodern" have, albeit grudgingly in many cases, become widely accepted as catchwords indicating the new sensibility, style, ethos, or disposition (de Alba 2000).

Perhaps another aspect from which the direction education has been motivated, at least in the 1980s and 1990s, is determined very much now by the taxpayer and what the taxpayer believes is essential. Coles

(1981) argues that the baby boom and other demographic changes are affecting education substantially due to

> the ageing of the population ... has been going on for more than two hundred years and now puts the median age at thirty-two ... an additional factor; the great increase in births around the year 1945 which temporarily reversed the declining birth rate (in America) that had been observed since 1800 ... The expansion of effort and energy (fiscal and social energy) to meet (these) demands is hardly available in the context of fighting for a bare-bones existence (Coles 1981).

Coles continues by arguing that education in the west since the mid-nineteenth century was increasingly made the province of governmental authorities and placed into increasingly complex organizations. Coles had therefore come to the conclusion that "now education is no longer a growth industry. If I had to analyze one trend that would continue... (and) affect education profoundly ... it would be these demographic realities" (ibid. 1981). It is with interest, although not within the scope of this book, that we could argue to oppose this last viewpoint if we were to consider the number of children in the world who, even today, have no access to formal schooling.

It is with this sociohistorical backdrop that we come to delve more specifically into the educational trends that have surfaced. These trends evolved also as a result of highly significant changes in society since World War II—changes which may also have their own built-in end or teleology). In effect, the purpose of this entire book is to consider those changes and attempt to deconstruct and revitalize the public education system to provide a way forward for the twenty-first century.

One can conjecture that adhering to a curriculum that allows for an input from various and different cultural perspectives will enhance a student's "other-cultural" awareness, a perspective that appears to be relevant for today's sociopolitical environment. One may also conjecture that this awareness will evolve if the student is exposed to peers of other cultures, or that exposure to other cultures or languages will produce an individual with skills to function in other cultural environments.

All of these statements are valid, but the factor which is most imperative is to coordinate these experiences for the student, while creating an innate awareness of the global culture in which the student will live. That means that the actual information that the student is taught is, as Bartlett (1996) points out, almost secondary in the student's academic development. In fact, the information serves more as a vehicle for delivering those curricular activities which may be less explicit than the formal curricular structure. This shifts the focus of curricular motivation further into the "why" arena instead of the "what" arena. This also means that we must give more thought to how to seamlessly weave the Hidden and Pastoral curricular structures into the academic curriculum, so that the educational outcome of these three structures is not conflictive. These aspects of the curriculum should be combined with an understanding of the other elements that comprise an institution, such as those outlined in the SPACE Factor (see Chapter 4). It is only then that we can conceive the motivational factors for a curriculum that promotes an international understanding and awareness through the academic thinking.

In his research on the international school environment, Thompson, in Hayden & Thompson (1998), supports the notion that learning within an institutional environment must be somehow given cohesiveness throughout. To help the reader visualize his conception, he utilizes what he terms the "brick wall" metaphor, where the learning environment can be broken down into bricks (subject learning) that are held together by mortar (what Thompson calls interstitial learning) to create the wall (whole institutional learning). The most interesting part to Thompson's model is the "interstitial learning" aspect which Thompson defines as "opportunities for (international) learning that takes place between the subjects of the curriculum, and that arises from the various styles of interdisciplinary and transdisciplinary processes that are part of the planned and unplanned experience for the students and teachers. Such 'interstitial learning' is likely to involve not only those academic subjects, but also to include learning associated with such structures as pastoral care, guidance, discipline codes, approaches to individual special needs, and what has become known as the hidden curriculum, all of which can make a contribution to the generation of an international attitude" (ibid. 1998). This author also believes that the concept of interstitial learning and related metaphors are just as valid for any academic institution that adheres to the acknowledged systemic framework outlined above. In any case, Thompson's analytical framework perhaps helps to shed more light on our present deconstruction process.

To proceed, individually it appears the individual elements found within an academic institutional setting do need specific attention in their design and makeup, but it is not until they have combined in an appropriate manner that the gestalt of the curriculum is achieved. In other words, the whole is greater than the sum of its parts—in this case those elements which comprise the SPACE Factor, the most relevant of which is the *C* that stands for the curriculum. The latter encompasses the relationship of the Academic, Hidden, and Pastoral curricular structures to the sociocultural paradigmatic structure, which results in the creation of a proactive educational environment that's relevant to the school's social environment. It becomes clear that catering to any hegemonic tendency within any of these three curricular frameworks provides little contribution to creating a contemporary-minded student who needs to prepare him or herself for tomorrow's society. In other words, if a more contemporary sociopolitical character is achieved through the careful interaction of the curricular pieces outlined above, then the prospects of delivering a relevant twenty-first-century education will be greatly enhanced in the self-appointed obligation to achieve our educational potential.

It is therefore imperative that educators are aware of those curricular "interstices" (see glossary for fuller explanation) and of the educational messages they communicate which, as Thompson suggests, are pertinent to the mission of education. Those who have entered education as a profession may have come to know the import of this almost inherently, but it would be amiss not to address more closely the requirements of these otherwise hidden curricular elements which may not necessarily be part of the recognized structure. In other words, the paradigmatic curricular structures, as outlined in Chapter 12, need to be more thoroughly addressed. Inability or unwillingness to address these fundamental issues of what constitutes the paradigm or "brick wall" would hinder the development of a contemporary educational mindset, resulting in an educational product that does not achieve the needs of the society it is meant to serve.

In summary, a subsequent descriptive curriculum that focuses on developing a proactive contemporary outlook, as opposed to one which is more prescriptive and entails specific instructions of how to achieve the specified goals, should be created. The focus would be on clarifying elements that have not been prescribed by the chosen curricular structures. This process would therefore provide general guidelines as to how to tackle the problem of creating an appropriate sociopolitical learning environment—one in which the student can thrive, learn from, and come out of better prepared than ever before.

Peter J. Zsebik, Ph.D.

DISCUSSION AND REVIEW QUESTIONS FOR CHAPTER 13

1. In your study groups, or in your notebook, comment on the different influences that were placed on curricular programs. Are there any aspects to these influences that appear to be common throughout?

2. According to de Alba, what is the prime purpose of curricular programming? Do you agree? Why?

3. Discuss other current sociopolitical trends that appear to be affecting public education. What challenges and/or opportunities do you see for public education, and how much change would be required to maintain its relevancy?

4. How does the notion of "interstitial learning" contribute to one's understanding of the connectedness between curricular programs?

CHAPTER 14

CURRICULUM DESIGN, IMPLEMENTATION, AND EVALUATION

In the twenty-first century, it is important to understand that the curricular structure is more than a hypothetical undertaking. It requires analyzing the design, implementation, and evaluation of the specified curriculum. It is no easy matter to analyze these three aspects, but nevertheless, understanding these three areas pose a constant struggle that hangs over the realm of education.

On a practical, everyday basis, it can be argued that there are as many different curricular design, implementation, and evaluation strategies as there are people who have the courage to write them down.

While it appears that there is no one way to design, implement, or evaluate a curricular structure, however, there do appear to be certain published ideas which may prove helpful in our understanding of the underlying principles.

DEFINING CURRICULAR OBJECTIVES

Although the following aspects focus primarily on curricular objectives based on a modernist notion, they nevertheless have their place in helping us understand more comprehensively the needs of education. It is not the intent of the book to displace what already exists, but rather to reconceptualize what is available, and to bring it more in line with the needs of present society. With this in mind, let us continue by summarizing some of the more pertinent research concerning curriculum. Indeed, some of the perspectives brought to light in the following overview may prove extremely useful as points of reference for the current social discourse that education must now address.

Davies (1994) believes that it is important for curriculum writers to be clear in their concept of what they want to achieve. He therefore begins with defining the following:

> *Aim*—a general statement which attempts to give both shape and direction to a set of more detailed intentions for the future.
>
> *Goal*—related to aims but more explicit in character; attempts to show the destination to which the learner must come.
>
> *Objective*—is highly explicit and operational in form, as well as timebound and quantifiable. (The objectives) attempt to describe in the clearest terms possible exactly what a student will think, act, or feel at the end of a learning experience.

Tyler (1949) begins his treatise on curriculum with the important concept that one needs to have clearly defined objectives, not only within the classroom, but also within the context of the school. He believes there are different sources that need to be taken into account when attempting to decide on the appropriate objectives, including:

- The study of the learners themselves
- The study of contemporary life outside school
- Suggestions about objectives from subject specialists
- The use of philosophy
- The use of learning psychology

Tyler concedes on all of the above that there are flaws to each process, and that none therefore should be used exclusively in developing objectives. Tyler also emphasizes that stating objectives in a form that is helpful to selecting learning experiences (and to help guide teaching) has just as much import as the selection process itself. According to Tyler, these objectives can take the form of prescriptive, descriptive, or generalist behaviour outcomes. Tyler adds, however, that objective outcomes must be more specific. "The most useful form for stating objectives is to express them in terms which identify both the kind of behaviour to be developed in the student and the context or area of life in which this behaviour is to operate" (Tyler 1949).

Hirst and Peters (1970) begin their analysis of curriculum planning by also citing the need for objectives, as follows:

> the planning of a curriculum, or any part of it, is (here) seen as a logical nonsense until the objectives being aimed at are made clear. At this general level statements of aims have to be translated into statements of specific objectives to which curriculum activities can be explicitly directed.

Hirst and Peters continue their analysis of curricular design by stating that one of the most essential aspects to curricular design and its relevant planning is the actual selection of objectives which they have formalized into two specific categories: a general versus a specialized educational structure. They define specialized education as a narrow limitation of the subjects to be studied, versus general education which allows for a large selection of subjects to be studied. The selection between these two structures will determine the educational outcome. Hirst and Peters believe that the general structure may hold more advantages than the specialized structure, and this, say the authors, is perhaps the reason why "it is not surprising that there is a persistent call that general education shall be maintained for all throughout the secondary school stage" (Hirst and Peters, 1970).

One additional important factor these authors have pointed out is the fact that it may be necessary to focus on developing a curricular structure that addresses inter-relational concepts between subject areas which are currently being taught as distinct modules. This, in turn, may lead to a reorganization of the traditional methods of curricular organization; including not only the "subject" organization but the school's schedules and timetabling as well.

Hass and Parkay (1993) have determined that there are four bases of the curriculum which can be used as a major source of guidance for decision making in curriculum planning and the planning of teaching (implementation). These four bases are:

- Social forces
- Human development
- The nature of learning
- The nature of knowledge and cognition

These authors indicate that throughout the history of curricular planning, there have been changes of emphasis on which particular basis is given more credence. They believe, however, that proper curricular design entails giving each area due consideration for its contribution to the overall structure.

Ayers and Schubert (1989) in *Curriculum Planning: A New Approach, sixth edition* (Hass & Parkay 1993) voice what they see to be the central question: "On what basis are the knowledge and values we deem worthwhile for students selected?" They believe the answer to this question lies in understanding three different orientations that have historically been utilized for curriculum design. These include:

The Intellectual Traditionalist: those who promote the teaching of great ideas (from the great books) as the most worthwhile educational enterprise.

The Social Behaviorist: those who are more deeply concerned with techniques of curriculum delivery— techniques involving broader questions of teaching methods, organizational patterns, and instructional materials that have the warrant of scientific investigation.

The Experientialist: those who focus on the kind and quality of reflective thinking that persons use in everyday life as they encounter and deal with the continuous flow of problems—learning from experience.

Bagley (1941) (also in Hass & Parkay 1993) argues the case for Essentialism (related to the Traditionalist perspective): the teaching only of essentials, which includes the arts of recording (not electronically), computing (not electronically) and measuring, or in other words the three Rs. On the other side, Kilpatrick (1941) argues for the case of Progressivism when planning a curricular structure. In this case, Progressivism can be associated more closely with the Experientialist concept mentioned above.

The above concepts are echoed somewhat in Davies (1994) who sees three perspectives that reflect developing educational thought within this past century. The following perspectives were used to determine curricular objectives. These are:

- *The classical approach:* This approach is reminiscent of Bagley (1941) and he cites Tyler (1949) as an example. This approach is characterized by efficiency, obedience, and the development of one understands within the bureaucratic system.
- *The romantic or humanist approach:* This approach is essentially learner centered; it appeals to freedom rather than efficiency as demonstrated by Maria Montessori.
- *The classical-romantic or modern Approach:* Davies cites this approach as not simply a compromise of the first two; he sees the process rather than the content or method as central to the explanation of behavior, a perspective which Bartlett (1996) echoed earlier.

Hirst and Peters (1970) outline what can be construed as a fourth perspective, which is also found in Davies's work:

- *The Neoclassical Approach,* which argues there are seven forms of knowledge that are useful for determining objectives. These include:
  1) Formal logic and mathematics
  2) Physical sciences
  3) Awareness and understanding of own and other minds (interpersonal)

4) Moral judgment and awareness (intrapersonal)
5) Aesthetic
6) Religious
7) Philosophical

From this conception, Hirst and Peters then propose two basic assumptions:

a) There is a clear distinction between a general and a specialized understanding of these seven domains.

b) A general education implies that all seven domains need to be included in the curriculum. Objectives must be identified by applying appropriate criteria and making judgments about priority.

Phenix (1964) echoes the concept of using the different intellectual domains as a source of identifying objectives. He suggests that the curriculum should address six fundamental patterns of meaning. These patterns include:

1. Symbolics - including language, mathematics, and various symbolic forms
2. Empirics - including sciences of the physical world
3. Aesthetics - including the various arts
4. Synoetics - personal knowledge (intrapersonal)
5. Ethics - moral meanings that express obligation rather than fact
6. Synoptics - concepts that are integrative, such as history, religion, and philosophy and combine the above realms of meaning

Phenix believes that a unitary philosophy and design of the curriculum should focus around realms of meaning for the following reasons:

- All intelligent decisions concerning what is to be included and excluded from the course of study require a comprehensive all-inclusive outlook.
- A person is an organized whole and not a collection of separate parts, and the curriculum should have a corresponding organic quality.
- Society is an integrated social structure much like the body, and a curriculum planned as a comprehensive design for learning contributes a basis for the growth of community.
- A comprehensive structure gives added significance to each of the separate parts of the curriculum. The value of a subject is enhanced by an understanding of its relationship with other subjects.

While the determination of objectives is an important place to begin, it has undergone several changes over the years. It does appear, however, that the various educational approaches suggested previously do overlap, and is even directed in some cases by individuals who are attempting to find a comprehensive direction for public education. It also appears that the various theorists agree on using different resources to determine curricular objectives, with the implication that there is no reliance on one particular approach in determining the needs of the curricular structure.

DEFINING THE CURRICULAR ORGANIZATION

Once objectives have been secured, "it is necessary to consider the procedures for organizing learning experiences into units, courses, and program(me)s" (Tyler, 1949). The organization of a curriculum must therefore be approached as a long-term plan. "Changes in ways of thinking, in fundamental habits, in major operating concepts...develop slowly (in the child). It is only after months and years that we are able to see major educational objectives taking marked concrete shape" (ibid.). With this in mind, Tyler cites a number of other variables that need to be taken into account. His approach can be summarized as follows:

A) Three Criteria for Effective Organization:

Continuity: the curriculum must build upon previous learning skills

Sequence: the curriculum must use and enhance skills with progressively more difficult or varied material

Integration: the curriculum should make reference to the other subjects from a horizontal standpoint

B) Organizing Threads

There is a need to have a thread or concept which can be used to weave or sew together a complete curricular structure which can run for the specified length of time the curriculum is to be implemented (e.g., throughout the year or from Kindergarten through Grade 12).

C) Organizing Elements

It is necessary to recognize that learning experiences need to be organized to achieve the three criteria mentioned above. The organization must be based on the needs and abilities of the learner.

D) Organizing Principles

Some of the organizing principles include the use of chronological sequencing, although according to Tyler, this is not always the most effective, increasing the breadth of application, increasing the range of activities, the use of description followed by analysis, the development of specific illustrations followed by broader and broader principles to explain these illustrations, and the attempt to build an increasingly unified world picture from specific parts to the whole.

E) Organizing Structure

Tyler (1949) breaks the organizational structure of a curriculum down into three levels:

- *The Largest level*—this includes specific subjects, broad fields, a core curriculum, and/or a comprehensive curricular structure
- *The Intermediate level*—courses organized as a sequence to a larger whole and short-term courses
- *The Low level*—this includes the lesson, the topic, or the unit

F) Organizing Process

Tyler also cites five steps to organizing a curriculum:

a) Agreement on the general scheme of organization—subjects, fields, core
b) Agreement on the general organizing principles—organizing material
c) Agreement on the kind of low level unit to be used—lesson, unit, etc.
d) Developing flexible plans or "source units" for the teacher
e) Using pupil-teacher planning for the particular activities carried on by a particular class.

While Tyler's explanation of events surrounding the design of the curriculum are lucid and appear to follow common sense, Davies (1976) instead begins by focusing on "The Largest level," which Tyler has outlined in his "Organizing Structure" area. He suggests using the Phenix concept (1964) of "domains" to create a "coherent system of ideas by which all the different parts of a curriculum can be identified and ordered."

Davies also cites the process of using a taxonomy such as Bloom's, demonstrating that the three domains of Bloom's taxonomy (cognitive, affective, psycho-motor) could be used as an organizational structure for curriculum design.

Interestingly enough, Davies points out that "any method of classification is built upon assumption, and no method can be value free...For this reason it is clearly foolish, if not irresponsible, to adopt a method of classification without first attempting to analyze the values implicit in the scheme." This last statement from Davies is perhaps one of the most important ideas we need to consider when attempting to design any curricular structure, including one for our contemporary society. It is imperative that we as educators constantly scrutinize the assumptions we have made and the methods we have used to implement the curriculum we have chosen. We need to be as fully aware as possible of the "value" implications which are a part of the scheme.

Marsh describes yet another approach to curriculum planning as evidenced by Walker (1972), who termed his findings as the Naturalistic model. The Naturalistic model has three steps to it:

a) *Platform*—where those who are to write the curriculum develop a consensus through postulation of theories, aims, images (preconceptions), and procedures
b) *Deliberation*—where alternatives and differences are aired or viewed
c) *Design*—the actual writing of the document and where alternatives are no longer entertained

Marsh proceeds, however to outline the advantages and disadvantages of this planning model. Its most notable advantage is that it portrays accurately what really happens, and its disadvantage is that it assumes there are considerable blocks of time available, and that everyone is enthusiastic and opinionated. This hearkens back to what was outlined previously concerning the interaction between the interested parties.

Marsh continues by stating that, "Careful planning and development are obviously important, but they count for nothing unless teachers are aware of the product and have the skills to implement the curriculum in their classrooms." Marsh maintains this vein by suggesting that too much responsibility is placed on the teacher when in actual fact the teacher doesn't have the authority. The other extreme is that an external authority has absolute control over what goes on in the classroom.

The realistic view of curricular implementation lies between these two. The implications that arise from this vantage are enormous. If curricular implementation does indeed fall somewhere in the middle, then what are the reasons for this middle-of-the-road premise? Is it sociologically driven? Is it bureaucratically driven? The answer to these questions may hold promise for understanding future directions for public education, and chiefly with the implementation of a second-order change concept that will be introduced in Chapter 15. In any case, perhaps the best way to sum up the process of curriculum implementation is with this quote:

> The voyage from the first identification of student needs to eventual learner-achievement is often stormy, but more good curricula sink without a trace on the shoals of implementation than at any other point (Pratt, 1980).

In other words, implementing a curriculum is based on how effectively you can convince those involved that it is the right thing to do (see Chapter 12).

EVALUATING THE CURRICULUM

Pratt (ibid.) outlines very specifically the five steps he believes are needed to evaluate a curriculum:

1. Conduct an internal evaluation
2. Produce a revised draft
3. Obtain expert approval
4. Obtain a confidential review
5. Produce a curriculum prototype

Once this prototype is developed, then it becomes time to try out the new curriculum. This is achieved first through pilot testing on a small scale and in relatively small chunks. Students should be made aware that it is the curriculum that's being tested and not themselves. Pratt points out that depending on the curricular content, it may be difficult to find volunteers. A further factor to remember is the need to remain objective during this stage, and not blame the volunteers if something doesn't work.

One thing which the author would also include is the moral or ethical obligation towards the student. This testing should not prove detrimental to the subject's overall academic performance, and all care must be taken to not unduly affect the individual being tested for the research. After the pilot testing stage, a field test (which is like a dress rehearsal) is implemented on a typical sample. "Field tests perform both experimental and political functions: they serve to evaluate and to build support for it"(Pratt 1980).

Pratt divides the evaluation process of a curricular structure into different areas, namely *effectiveness, acceptability, and efficiency.* To evaluate the program's effectiveness, the crucial question is, "Did the minimum expected number of students achieve the minimum stipulated objectives at the minimum level?" It is also just as important that the program be acceptable. "A program that achieves all its objectives can still be a failure if the people involved disliked the experience." The third factor is efficiency. The central question in this area is whether the outcome of a program justifies the resources it has consumed.

Other questions which Pratt (ibid.) lists as essential when evaluating a curriculum include the following:

1. Is the curriculum meeting the needs of the community it is serving?
2. Are the aims and objectives apparent, recognized, accepted and significant?
3. Is student evaluation congruent, complete, objective, reliable, and efficient?
4. Are the prerequisites to enter the program in line with program expectations?
5. Are the content and methods consistent with the curriculum?
6. Are there provisions for different learning styles, learning speeds, and abilities?
7. Are materials and facilities specified in the curriculum available and used effectively? Are members of the faculty competent, and are costs in line with budget expectations?

Nixon (1992) suggests that evaluation of a curriculum can be placed into certain phases:

1. Planning, setting up, and focusing
2. Gathering evidence
3. Analyzing and disseminating findings
4. Utilizing findings

In general, Nixon believes that evaluation of a curriculum is a long-term process that must be understood to have an impact on the situation. The prime purpose of evaluation is to promote critical self-reflection and to produce accountability for what is being taught. Nixon also believes that one of the best ways to know if the curriculum is doing what it has set out to do is to use attitudinal surveys, and to deliver these surveys to the student:

> Given the current emphasis on increased pupil participation and negotiation, it is, as Richard Hazelwood (1990) points out, "remarkable that few attempts are being made systematically to examine pupils' attitudes to schooling."

The reason this may not be happening as often as he would like is because it may be too intrusive and too time consuming. Nixon, however, advises to keep three things in mind—the three Rs—when contemplating such a survey:

- *Readability*—the pupils must understand the question
- *Reliability*—the items in the questionnaire must yield reliable information that is relevant to the enquiry
- *Replicability*—the questionnaire should be such as to allow different groups, or the same group, later to answer the questions without need for a change.

McCormick and James (1990) echo Nixon's idea that the prime purpose of a curriculum evaluation is to provide accountability, and accountability is becoming more of a concern because of "the fragmentation of community" (Atkin 1979). The growth of single interest groups, the loss of confidence in specialists, and "anxiety over the apparent failure of education to deliver a variety of goods" may all be regarded as manifestations of the weakening of a common purpose (McCormick and James, 1990). What this means is that we demand accountability because there is a lack of common agreement which in turn creates distrust in the public eye. Nevertheless, accountability is still necessary, and can be found in three forms:

- *Answerability* (moral accountability) to student and parent
- *Responsibility* (professional accountability) to colleagues
- *Accountability* (contractual accountability) to employers and the political masters

McCormick and James continue with the notion that those who do the evaluation must have some credibility. Lack of credibility makes the whole process useless. This is aggravated by the fact that the "distrust" already mentioned is sometimes more frequent in practice than in theory. For instance, the authors have demonstrated that evaluation is done by two main groups of people: the Outsiders (people who are not part of what is being evaluated per se), and the Insiders (those who are part of what is being evaluated). In a national system, outside evaluation can attract hostile reactions when it is done by individuals who are not directly linked to the process being evaluated. This is especially true if the credibility of the individual doing the evaluation is at odds with those on the inside. Insider evaluation, however, is according to the authors, probably more conducive to curriculum improvement.

Within the teaching profession, the general feeling is that the greater the degree of autonomy that can be given to teachers and schools, the more likely they are to accept responsibility for education provision and become committed to improving its quality (McCormick and James 1990).

A SUMMARY OF CURRICULAR CONSTRUCTION

The notion of structuralism appears to be prevalent throughout this discussion concerning curriculum, from Gibson's structural analysis to de Alba's grand narratives discussed previously. As we will see, this book aims to produce a snapshot of public education, utilizing the four elements proposed by Gibson (see Chapter 9). *The Structures of Social Organization* and *the Structures of Human Competence* are defined by the SPACE Factor and their underlying political influences, while *The Structures of Thought* and *The Structures of Feeling* are defined by the outcomes of the research instrument being utilized. It can be argued as well that a school, like government, can only be defined as a structuralist frame within a postmodernist environment simply because it can only exist within a specified framework. Any attempt to isolate the necessary elements would place the school out of context, as it is this context which actually defines the school. In effect, the school institution is for education what government is for big business—a mythical (in Barthes's sense of the word) manifestation of a social imperative that uses structuralist designs to teach the necessities of living within the same social fabric which drives its own existence.

DISCUSSION AND REVIEW QUESTIONS FOR CHAPTER 14

1. Create a comparison table outlining the central features of the included curricular theorists and their ideas for curricular design. Are there any commonalities that appear to exist between these theorists' concepts?

2. After reviewing the different theories of curricular organization, outline the ones that would be most effective for today's contemporary educational environment.

3. Discuss the quote from Davies regarding the implications for educational change as found on page 173: *"any method of classification is built upon assumption, and no method can be value free .... For this reason it is clearly foolish, if not irresponsible, to adopt a method of classification without first attempting to analyze the values implicit in the scheme."*

4. Discuss the challenges facing the implementation of a new curricular design. How might they best be overcome?

5. List the elements of what must be kept in mind for a thorough evaluation of a curricular programme design?

6. List some of the notions to keep in mind for an effective evaluation within the educational system. What are some of the pitfalls to be aware of?

7. Outline the argument for a school to be placed within a structuralist philosophical frame. Can it be justified otherwise?

Chapter 15

First- and Second-Order Change in Education and Its Implications for Future Directions

Reviewing the Current Educational Paradigm

In an effort to frame this discussion, it is necessary to first review some of the ideas and concepts already introduced during the course of this book. It is likely that the ideas are now familiar and obvious, but in the end these last chapters have only served to provide the framework for our current discussion.

To know the system of education intimately, one must achieve a certain understanding of the processes inherent in the system. Perhaps the most important process affecting education is the sociopolitical changes in which the system is embroiled. These dynamic processes, at times undefined, unyielding, and complex are also in a constant state of flux; the process is now recognized as postmodernism (see Chapter 9). To review, Appadurai (see Chapter 6) describes the complexity of this environment through what he labels as five cultural flows, and these cultural flows are determining the directions and decisions of our society. He considers these different flows as reaching tidal proportions, to the extent that the control society has over itself is in danger of complete erosion. This is grandiose in its implication, and it obviously includes the impact these flows have on public education. If we bring our minds to bear on these narratives, it then becomes clear how vulnerable the system of education is to the many pressures and changing values that are constantly developing in society.

Is our society the same today as it was ten years ago? Some may say that our society has been changing daily, while others may point to a specific date in the calendar saying that this was the day the world and therefore our society truly changed. In every case, it would be hard to argue that society has not undergone change.

What of the education system, the process that was put in place by our society to prepare young people for that society? Has it changed? Again some may say that the educational system, too, is developing to maintain its currency with the surrounding sociopolitical environment. Educators have attempted to maintain relevancy by changing or developing a number of practices and standards favorable to the needs of the surrounding society. However, others may come to the conclusion that today's public education environment has reached a level of maturity in its present form that is hindering the further development needed to render it consistent with the surrounding sociopolitical environment. This sense can be evidenced by persistent quests to understand how best to quantify, to qualify, or even to legitimate current systemic expressions as an effective educational process. Indeed, to reiterate, Michael Fullan has stated in his Change Forces series of publications (see Fullan 2003) that to more fully appreciate today's educational environment, one must now turn to complexity theory to understand the intricacies now apparent in, and for, the system (see Chapter 2). It would seem that the beginning of the twenty-first century may have left many educator's scratching their head over our current educational paradigm; an uncertainty articulated by the ever-mounting pressures placed on educators. The series of unanswered questions has only increased over time—questions that concern public education's role as an effective mediator for learning and socialization for the twenty-first century.

A search for a process that encourages social and educational development is not new to education. In fact, the very introduction of public education to our society marked the beginning of an ongoing struggle to create an idyllic social framework (see Chapter 12 for Lawton). Educators in the past have demonstrated apparent ingenuity and resilience in addressing the epistemological implications for society's philosophical transitions from industrialization to modernism to postmodernism. In the process they have managed to maintain the required institutional character of the educational construct. It even appeared that postmodernism (see Chapter 9) and its allusions would be tackled with some technological additions to the school environment, coupled albeit with a perhaps subliminal acknowledgement that education was no longer fully able to complete the task of a child's perceived educational need, and therefore was perhaps the reason that the idea of facilitation rather than of teaching the student emerged. Instead, a subtle change in focus materialized, primarily after the Second World War, with the notion that primary and secondary public education was now simply a precursor to tertiary education and training before full acceptance into society. Pundits encouraged the process by insisting that the world has become ever more complex, and to be successful it was necessary to continue one's education well beyond previous formerly acceptable time frames.

If we are in a changing age of social discourse, however, then is it still appropriate for us to continue to impose a modernist approach on those who will live and work in a postmodernist environment?

Is the school a modernist environment? A brief tour of a school will effectively demonstrate that the only real change that has occurred for the last century within the teaching profession is primarily cosmetic: the use of individual plastic chairs and desks instead of benches, various writing and display technologies, the types of punishment being utilized, and the added rights and restrictions of the child. Indeed it would be hard to find something going on in a school that did not have some historical referencing; classroom interaction is still primarily teacher-driven, product oriented, and factory organized.

In fact, some may make the case that the only real changes that have occurred within the educational environment in the last few decades is the way students are perceived as individuals in our society. In his extensive overview of childhood and adolescence, Epstein (2007) sees our current sociopolitical perspective on this demographic as an artificial construct that was created due to a number of social influences, including the ethical mindset of the western culture at the beginning of the twentieth century. This mindset resulted in a dramatic increase in:

- The creation of unheard of numbers of restrictive laws for young people
- The organization of labor unions to protect union members' jobs by restricting the access for young people to places of work
- Mandatory schooling for children and teenagers as a form of social control.

This raises the question as to whether our current perception for school is accurate. Do students really need to be in school as long as they are to achieve success? Or is it a necessity that educators perceive to prolong the educational experience so that the complexities of the world may be properly addressed? Or are current school environments a continuation of a social model that may not be as effective as it was viewed historically but was found easier to continue due to lack of choice, of alternative, or of economic imperative? Indeed, it is of note that the economic imperative issue appears to have driven political decision making in areas such as California who will be switching to the four day school week. If the economic imperative does holds precedence, then it is easy to see that our current educational paradigm and the incremental changes that perpetuate it may not be enough to hold the hounds of change at bay. This in turn implies that a time may come when our current educational paradigm is no longer adequately serving the society where it resides.

There is ample evidence of this need for change in the everyday occurrences within the academic environment. A cursory observation of the technological and historical narratives that are enveloping our world, and the way we attempt to interact with these narratives within education (as exemplified by the sometimes inadequate use of new technologies) does appear to indicate public education's weakness for addressing real-time sociopolitical change.

De Alba (2000) concurs with this analysis, stating that:

> many of the former social subjects are barely recognizable in the terms we had known them previously, and in some cases their very legitimation is in question...(this can lead to) the emergence of social traits and contours out of which new hegemonic practices can be articulated.

De Alba suggests that this particular item is noteworthy for this context because she believes that any inability to address change would probably also result in a reversion to hegemonic tendencies or maintenance of the status quo (see Chapter 10). It would therefore appear that the educational constructs necessary to encourage critical thinking and problem solving would in turn provide contributions to the development of paradigm-changing solutions. It is more probable, however, that within the confines of current public education institutions, there would be little observable impetus for addressing the grand narrative discrepancies that surround the educational paradigm. And if such initiatives were implemented, then the next question would be: what level of change is being utilized to initiate these changes?

As educators we are constantly trying to improve upon the level of service that we provide to our clientele. The unfortunate thing is that as educators we may be submerged by the demands of the job and our own historical experience as a product of the same system. It is exceedingly hard to see something if one doesn't know what to look for, or even that something different exists. Perhaps it is for this reason that the state of education and our inability to effect real change within the system has a sense of being unobtainable.

FIRST- AND SECOND-ORDER CHANGE AS A PROCESS FOR EDUCATIONAL REFORM

Interestingly, a new form of dialogue has begun to appear within education—a dialogue that may break the current cyclical nature of playing catch-up to society in which education is entwined (see Zsebik 2003). This in turn may encourage a lasting transformation that would prove beneficial to both current and future educational processes. It centers on the notion of first-order and second-order change, a process that provides a new discourse for creating answers to perennial problems that constantly resurface within the system of education. In effect, it is creating a new paradigm for leadership within the educational paradigm.

To begin this discussion, Maier (1987) defines first- versus second-order change and concludes with the following statement:

> First-order change is incremental, a linear progression to do more or less, better, faster, or with greater accuracy. Practice, reinforcement, and time will be the most likely approaches for facilitating sound developmental change of this kind. Activities are tangible, usually verbal interactions between the caregiver and the young person involved.

> Second-order change, on the other hand, involves a nonlinear progression, a transformation from one state to another. The aim would be to enable the individual to behave, think, or feel differently. Within the second-order change approach, applicable practice tools might be modeling, confrontation, conflict work, refraining and, most important, the introduction of decisively different personal experience over time. A crucial task of care workers is to be clear as to which order of change they are striving to create" (Maier 1987).

It is noteworthy that Maier perceives second-order change as the process that creates the most conflict, possibly through the inclusion of personal experience and legitimation of the individual. This is much different than the first order he describes. In a first-order change, the change occurs when the individual changes to conform to the order into which he or she is placed. Second-order change, on the other hand, seemingly embraces the individual and his or her talents or experiences and attempts to positively incorporate them into the process, without diminishing that person's input.

If we look further, we see that according to Waters, et al. (2003), first-order change can be defined as:

> changes that are consistent with existing values, norms (that) create advantages for individuals or stakeholder

groups with similar interests, (it) can be implemented with existing knowledge and resources, and where agreement exists on what changes are needed and on how the changes should be implemented...

It is apparent that Waters et al. believe first-order change to be rooted in what is already known or instituted. Waters et al. then proceed to give examples such as new classroom instructional practices, instructional materials, curriculum programs, or data collection and reporting systems that build on established patterns, knowledge, and practices.

Second-order change according to Waters et al. (ibid.), can be defined as when:

A change ... is not obvious (as to) how it will make things better for people with similar interests, (and) it requires individuals and groups of stakeholders to learn new approaches, or it conflicts with prevailing values and norms

As we can see from these definitions, the notion of first- and second-order change primarily relies on the eye of the beholder, and as we have observed, it can be the crux of much conflict, a possibility that always exists whenever a number of reasonably intelligent individuals are working towards a published common goal. As well, when different perceptions about the implications for a change are understood, there is inevitably the result that what one may perceive as a first-order change may be perceived by another as a second-order change—in other words what one may see as a solution may, to another, be a problem, and vice versa. From a pedagogical perspective, it seems that this dichotomy of thought would need to be the focus for any leader willing to take on a second-order change process.

To continue, Waters et al. (ibid.) then make an admirable comparison between what they believe are the differences that characterize first- and second-order change as shown in the following table:

First Order Change	Second Order Change
An extension of the past	*A break with the past*
Within existing paradigms	*Outside existing paradigms*
Consistent with prevailing values and norms	*Conflicted with prevailing values and norms*
Focused	*Emergent*
Bounded	*Unbounded*
Incremental	*Complex*
Linear	*Nonlinear*
Marginal	*A disturbance in every element of the system*
Implemented with existing knowledge skills	*Requires new knowledge and skills to implement*
Problem and Solution-oriented	*Neither problem nor solution-oriented*
Implemented by experts	*Implemented by stakeholders*

Fig 15.1 – *Overview of First- and Second-order change by Waters and Grubb (2004)*

If we start to explore the different types of relationships existing within the educational environment, it becomes easy to see the types of relationships that exist and perhaps to what specific order of change these relationships belong. The following is a listing of potential relationships that have been discerned as evident within an educational framework:

First Order Focus	Second Order Focus
Administrative decision making	*Collaborative teacher administrative decision making*
Hegemonic curriculum (taught with idea of maintaining the status quo)	*Transformative curriculum (taught with change in mind)*
Societal expectations with historical roots	*Societal expectations based on prognosis for future needs*
Teacher as information banker	*Teacher as information facilitator*
Student as passive recipient of information	*Student as active manager of information*
Curriculum focused on first order skill sets	*Curriculum focused on second order skill sets*
Parents and family as 'arm's length' participants of child's education (factory model)	*Parents and family as full participants of child's education (village model)*

Fig 15.2 – *Potential Relationships in Education*

While some obvious features become apparent once a definition has been brought forward, it is still important to note that these definitions are still only broadly defining an otherwise complex process. In fact this process, while perhaps fruitful, may be full of potentially explosive obstacles and traps if it is not treated with the utmost care. An example of a negative consequence could be the initiation of a pseudo second-order change process, which in reality is a first-order change process that results in very little beneficial development.

With this in mind, we therefore find that Waters, Marzano, and McNulty (2003) make an attempt to demonstrate that in order for second-order change to occur, we must balance the latter change levels with the needed first-order change levels, and the most effective way to encourage this process is through the use of appropriate leadership practices. The authors suggest that to begin from only a second-order perspective would probably hamper any benefits that the change may otherwise bring. The authors then continue by listing the administration's responsibilities when attempting to change the culture of a school:

1. Promotes cooperation among staff
2. Promotes a sense of well-being
3. Promotes cohesion among staff
4. Develops a shared understanding of purpose
5. Develops a shared vision of what the school could be like

Following this listing of responsibilities, the authors then postulate that for first-order changes, the first three practices listed above are:

> all that is needed from leadership for successful implementation.
>
> However, for second-order changes these first three practices will be insufficient to fulfill this responsibility. Second-order changes require leaders to work far more deeply with staff and the community" (ibid. p.8).

From this vantage it appears likely that second-order change will only occur through the willing participation of teachers and those who are in the classroom. The only problem is that teachers today have perhaps focused their teaching efforts towards their own perception of educational needs which (due to no fault of their own) are often rooted in historical tradition and perception of classroom needs. When teachers face numerous other challenges in any given academic setting, it is also possible that the idea of second-order change would take a backseat to the more everyday pressing issues of classroom management, political intrigues, organizational and bureaucratic tasks, and the responsibilities accompanying daily living in a complex society. In brief, there could be so much resistance that the whole process would eventually be scuttled. This is likely to happen unless teachers have received proper and inspirational leadership to help them recognize and understand the idea of second-order change.

It would appear that a change of this magnitude would only occur if there was a leadership paradigm that was not only aware of the existing sociopolitical environment, but that also had a clear and unwavering vision of the process necessary to enact or create this needed shift into a more advantageous second-order paradigm—a paradigm that would address the needs of today's sociopolitical and socioeducational context.

Marzano (Winter 1995), however, postulates that innovations must fit within individuals' beliefs and perceptions. He believes that to affect such change, the Concern Based Adoption Model, or CBAM, created by Hall and Loucks (1978) may provide a way forward. This model defines seven stages or phases "individuals progress through as they become aware of, understand, and then gradually accept and then apply an innovation." (Marzano 1995) These stages are:

Stage 1 *Awareness:* participants exhibit little awareness about the innovation

Stage 2 *Informational:* participants exhibit an awareness of the innovation and a desire for more information about the innovation

Stage 3 *Personal:* participants are uncertain about the demands of the innovation and are concerned about how it will affect their lives

Stage 4 *Management:* participants have basically "accepted" the innovation as useful and are concerned about accurately and effectively utilizing the innovation

Stage 5 *Consequences:* participants are concerned about the impact of the innovation on their clients (i.e., commonly students within education) and their work in general

Stage 6 *Collaboration:* participants' concerns are focused on coordination and cooperation with others regarding the innovation

Stage 7 *Refocusing:* participants' concerns are focused on improving the innovation and identifying other uses of the innovation

Hall and Loucks (1978) in Marzano (1995)

These developmental stages could pose a satisfactory canon from which to attempt a second-order change, but with the caveat that before any change can be affected, all parties involved must believe and perceive that change is necessary to allow its full integration. If the change is not accepted fully, then the process fails.

As we have seen, the notion of change seems to go hand-in-hand with education, but in this instance, the idea is that the way to bring about change within this environment is through a much more democratic arrangement. This means that in order to effectively create a second-order changed environment all stakeholders within the system must be involved in the process. Still, it may be to all intents that initiation of any such process will need to occur at the administrative level. That means then that if the process is to proceed past the initial stages, then it will be incumbent on the initiators to proceed through all the stages cited above to ensure that the process is accepted and that the necessary beliefs and perceptions are transferred. Only then would there be a guarantee of success with the proscribed change.

Discussion and Review Questions for Chapter 15

1. Discuss the elements of education that appear to have changed this sociopolitical environment. Create a chart listing changes of the past as useful, innovative, technologically-driven, faddish, challenging, or ineffective. Feel free to add more elements if necessary. Are there any commonalities found within your lists?

2. What sociopolitical elements seemingly prevent or slow change in public education?

3. Independently contemplate your own past knowledge premise. Is it focused on maintaining the systemic structure that has been inherited or on attempting to create a more contemporary educational paradigm?

4. What appear to be the essential elements for any second-order change to occur? As an administrative leader, how would you encourage these elements to work together?

5. Discuss in your group some of the challenges that may exist for a second-order change dialectic to be successful. Share your list with others and discuss.

6. Draw up a list of changes that you believe could be made to education to make it better aligned with your perception of our contemporary society. Take note of the following:
   • Which items you feel should be discarded
   • Which items you feel should be included
   • Which items you feel should stay the same.

Be prepared to justify your answers.

CHAPTER 16

INTERVENTION—A POTENTIAL FRAMEWORK FOR INTRODUCING SECOND-ORDER CHANGE INTO AN EDUCATIONAL ENVIRONMENT

Once we understand the issues relating to educational change, as has been outlined in past chapters, a sense will emerge that the educational paradigm is not merely a bureaucratic behemoth that must be managed. Instead, it may be helpful to realize the system of education as more organic in nature. This notion is in line with Neville's notion (see Chapter 4) that sees the educational environment as a garden that we must maintained. Indeed, since the very idea of an academic institution can only exist by adding organic elements (such as people), then is it not logical to approach this argument as an organic predicament rather than a managerial problem? This outlook may indeed serve a way forward for public education in the twenty-first century.

If we are to bring substantial and sustainable changes into our contemporary public education systems, then that change should not metaphorically throw the baby out with the bathwater. Instead, we must incorporate a "baby steps" incremental change approach toward a more contemporary systemic structure.

In other words, the administrative leadership of a school (or other institutional organization) must find opportunities that may already exist, and then it must take steps to incorporate incremental change towards a future goal in its everyday development. The important step, however, is to recognize these opportunities, and to create the right environment for a successful systemic intervention.

The interesting, or what we may call symptomatic aspect, of a *successful* systemic intervention is that it will feed on itself, generating other opportunities and symbiotic relationships that will build on the successes of the past, in (as has been already noted) an approximate equivalent to organic development. This also implies that any systemic intervention we incorporate must be considered a longitudinal concept— which basically means that development and maintenance of a second-order change environment must be secured by long-term planning, and most especially by a long-term commitment to the plan.

As has been noted in this book, there are many complexities and obstacles to creating, developing, and maintaining a long term systemic intervention that bears a difference, not only in the quality of the appropriate ideological focus, but also in the quantity of the appropriate methodological and curricular focus. It is for this reason that the more parties involved in the process, the more successful the systemic intervention will be. If all of these things are taken into account, the result will be a permanent systemic change for the educational environment that is beneficial to our twenty-first-century society.

The diagram in Figure 12.3 provides a point of organizational departure that shows the *Model of Socio-Political Influence on Curricular Creation in Education,* This model has several advantages: it provides a basic breakdown of the system inherent in the educational structure, and it allows the flexibility needed to incorporate second-order elements into the specified system. Another advantage is that the model can be used as a "road map" that outlines the linear logical process that any new ideological perspective must undergo before it is accepted and adopted in the educational environment.

It is also interesting to note that the possible results of the sociopolitical choices available to the educational environment are also clearly defined by the educational results exhibited by the students. In turn, this factor would help leaders to focus on the type of sociopolitical environment they want to initiate as part of their second-order change process. In fact, if educational leaders were to redefine the roles of those SPACE elements utilizing second-order change ideals in the chosen institution as outlined in Chapter 15, it follows that the sociopolitical landscape of the environment would also change. This would then be followed by the creation of a new curricular paradigm that incorporates second-order change concepts, and so on. The final result in this case is, hopefully, a metamorphosis of a curricular environment that promotes the chosen sociopolitical environment. Let us hope that the latter environment is of a transformative nature, as we can now believe that this is the only appropriate focus for today's environment.

A FIVE–STAGE GUIDE FOR INCORPORATING SECOND-ORDER CHANGE IN AN INSTITUTION

From a practical side, a program of change requires leaders to undertake detailed planning before they attempt a change in institutions, especially if the change is as dichotomous as a second-order change. Established sociopolitical environments may be particularly resistant to change, even if they are in need of a paradigmatic shift in program focus. Developing any change process in an established community is not for the faint of heart. The process can be long and challenging, but the rewards for the entire sociopolitical environment would be enormous, and the educational outcome (the students) of that institution would be better prepared for the twenty-first-century society in which they will work and live. In effect, this change process will benefit all parties involved in the sociopolitical environment.

One more thing that needs to be said is that change of any sort requires time and patience. In many a bureaucratic case, change is not symbiotic with current educational management practices, so it is incumbent on leaders to establish the appropriate environmental setting. This setting may have to be somewhat insulated from any constant management restructuring that has been encouraged or even enforced by higher management circles who may currently be treating a constant re-shifting of individuals as a best practices process. While it may be helpful in some cases to enforce short-term restructuring at management and leadership levels, this constant restructuring can also be a double-edged sword, whereby any new initiatives that are attempted and developed at one location often fail after the initiating leadership has been moved to another physical location. In any case, a progressive leader should also take into account a secondary process within the change orientation process. The latter involves how to create a culture of second-order change that will continue even after that particular initializing leadership has moved on. Of course, the best way to ensure the continuance of second-order change is to train and encourage leaders to develop this process at all levels of the systemic structure, so that second-order change encompasses every sociopolitical environment found within the system. Indeed, if the system adopts a second-order change process, then the entire restructuring of school settings becomes much more feasible.

Here then is a guideline that may be useful for educational leaders when incorporating change practices into their institutional setting. Below you will find a five stage process for change and within each of these five stages is a seven step action plan procedure that will help guide you through each stage as you incorporate change in your school environment.

The Seven Steps to Aid in Developing your Action Plan for each Stage:

1. Creation of data collection instrument or process
2. Development of data collection instrument
3. Distribution
4. Collection
5. Collation of results
6. Data analysis
7. Reporting to the community of the results

The Five-Stage Process to Creating Change in your Educational Institution:

STAGE ONE: ORGANIZE YOUR CHANGE PROCESS

Organize a comprehensive process for collecting data from beginning to end. The following seven steps provide an effective framework for organizing your Action Plan. A detailed and organized plan is essential when attempting to incorporate new ideals and philosophical perspectives into your school environment. These seven steps are cumulative steps so that the most effective procedure is to build on the data and information obtained from the previous steps.

Designate individuals in your school who can help with this seven step action plan. They don't have to be the same people, unless there is no other way to provide the needed continuity to establish validity of the results. It is also important to remember that the effort to incorporate change must be balanced with the work and stress loads already affecting the individuals you are relying on.

The seven step action plan detailed above should apply to each change process stage that requires data to justify its effectiveness, acceptance, and continuance as part of the sociopolitical environment.

STAGE TWO: UNDERSTAND YOUR SPACE ENVIRONMENT

- *Know the individuals* that you can count on in your sociopolitical environment, and identify those who may resist any change.
- *Develop a comprehensive understanding* of the needs and wants of the community, possibly through surveys, informal interviews, staff meetings, and school council meetings. As has already been noted, to more fully create a complete picture of your school environment, you need to include all parties in the data-collection process. It is only then that you will be able to achieve that comprehensive picture necessary to design a plan for change in your school.

STAGE THREE: UNDERSTAND YOUR CURRENT SOCIOPOLITICAL ENVIRONMENT

- *Develop a comprehensive perspective* of the social dynamics inherent to your particular institution by attempting a mind map that outlines the connections between the different parties.
- *Develop a diagnostic assessment of your school* (done perhaps through a survey for each of those elements found in SPACE), an analysis of your mission statement, school plan,

and conduct informal interviews with various interested parties.

- *Determine what incentives ("carrots") are needed* to entice people to accepting and working for the change process. Often all that is required is to describe the benefits that are inherent in adopting a second-order change perspective.
- *Organize workshops for all parties* in the school (think SPACE) to provide them with the necessary information for an informed decision.
- *Determine any budgetary requirements* (if any) to facilitate any justifiable change process.
- *Determine any scheduling requirements* or challenges.
- *Stick with your plans* to introduce second-order change elements, BUT:
- *Always allow flexibility in your planning.* To know that your plans are taking effect, you should incorporate the same successful managerial methods that you currently use, including strategic planning, staff meetings, institutional incentives, and other necessary leadership driven practices (to get the horse moving).

STAGE FOUR: MAINTAIN CONSISTENCY IN YOUR PROGRAM DEVELOPMENT

- *Regularly schedule meetings*, possibly using a central committee composed of chosen leaders who report on the progress of their designated subcommittees
- *Set feasible targets for incorporation of changes.* A little time crunch can go a long way in creating a motivational situation, but these targets should be created by the personnel the changes affect. This also encourages interested parties to more fully accept the process by achieving an ownership and collaborative decision-making mentality (both of these ideas have been found to be second-order process imperatives).

STAGE 5: EVALUATE AND ASSESS THE PROCESS

- *Determine a specific time frame* for incorporation of new strategies.

- *Run an evaluative assessment* at the end of your specified time frame. The assessment would be perhaps similar in design to that which you had already designed for your *diagnostic assessment* process, keeping in mind that now would be the occasion to be more specific with your assessment process regarding specific areas.
- *Initialize a redefining process* through collaboration with the parties that are involved in that process. Questions that may prove helpful include:
  1. What happened?
  2. What was the cause of the lack of success?
  3. What could be done differently?
  4. Can the process in question be treated differently to ensure success?
  5. Is there anything in the process worth holding on to?

CONCLUSION

It must be stressed once more that this reorganization does not necessarily entail a starting-from-scratch mentality. Indeed, many of the bureaucratic tools already in place in public education (scheduling, budgeting, etc.) simply have to achieve a different organizational process other than the traditional hierarchical approach. This can be accomplished by using an enriched, shared vocabulary that is initiated throughout the education environment, while simultaneously creating differently defined communicative processes between the interested parties.

This author firmly believes that now is the time for educational leaders to take the initiative to enact change for the system of public education. This book is not meant to provide all the answers. Instead it is a book that is meant to initiate the process of thinking that is conducive to preparing a mindset for educational change. This author's experience of not only teaching students but also of teaching teachers within the system of mass education has allowed for a full spectrum of cognitive understanding that is now being realized in print form. It is hoped that your own journey of educational enquiry will result in a similar spectrum of success and understanding that will culminate in a reaffirmation of a purpose-driven educational career. Good luck and good leading.

And remember! Don't try to attempt this alone. **Education is *of* the community and *for* the community, so it should be *by* the community!**

Sound familiar? Good luck!

DISCUSSION AND REVIEW QUESTIONS FOR CHAPTER 16

Create a rough draft of how you might incorporate the *The Five-Stage Process to Creating Change in your Educational Institution* into your educational environment. Be sure to also sketch the Seven-step Action Plan Procedure in some detail for each of the stages.

Refer to the previous chapters for guidance and motivational arguments.

GLOSSARY

For terms not mentioned in the glossary, see the Index.

Accommodating intellectual This is an individual who is aware of the needs, problems, and opportunities of his environment, but he attempts very little to affect change due to his belief that nothing will change.

Applicable Something that is capable of being applied or that is intended to apply.

Banking Education A term coined by Paolo Freire in the 1970s to describe his observations of the education system in Brazil. His observations focused on the interactions between teachers and students. It describes the process where the teacher "deposits" information into the students for them to remember and repeat with no opportunity for critical thinking. The information "deposited" is very basic and these educational decisions, he argues, are taken as a political tool to prevent critical thinking from occurring, and this is done to maintain the political power structures already in place in the society.

Binary Opposition (see Structuralism)

Continuum (of Interaction) A process of different elements acting on each other usually through many stages or levels and possibly resulting in a final expanded outcome that has developed considerably from its beginnings. In this case the experiences or developments that occur throughout this interactive process build on each other, much like when certain ingredients are placed together to undergo a baking process that result in a loaf of bread.

Critical intellectual This is an individual who has received the necessary skills and information to identify the problems and opportunities in his environment. However, his criticism falls short of action. He lacks the impetus or intellectual scope to affect serious change.

Cultural Relativism An educational doctrine that could be adopted where the focus is not on teaching certain cultural norms and values and ignoring or dismissing others, but rather on encouraging more equitable relationships and partnerships between cultures.

Deconstruction A process that breaks down a physical space or a mental concept to its essential parts. This process is useful for analyzing the elements of the specified space or concept.

Educational Dialectic A term used to label the combined interactions, patterns, and organizations which help to identify and analyze accepted theories and practices of mass education.

Ethos A term used to describe the spirit or character that is found within an insititutaional environment or system. It is often expressed through the culture, philosophical orientation, and a general way of thinking that is perceptible to outside observers. An ethos can be analyzed through the interactions and decision-making processes that have been identified in the environment or system.

First Order Change used to define a linear progression of development in society established by the power structures in place. Within the context of education, First Order Change is characterized by current bureaucratic patterns and traditions of system organization.

Gestalt A German word used to describe the idea that the whole is greater than the sum of the parts that has been identified.

Hegemonic A term used to describe the dominance or leadership of one state, nation, or culture (ideology). This is sometimes accomplished through exclusion or forced conformity of minority or weaker elements to the dominant culture.

Hegemonic Intellectual (see Hegemonic Paradigm) A label for one who has only managed to adopt limited relationships with the dominant group due primarily to restricted access to information which in turn helps to maintain the status quo of the dominant group.

Hegemonic Paradigm See paradigm.

Interaction A term used to describe the dynamic influence and actions surrounding a certain an institution or environment that in turn helps to define the character of that institution.

International A term used to describe relations between states that express solidarity and equality between the different states.

Interstitial A label that identifies the (small) space between two things or elements.

Interstitial Culture A label that identifies that which is created, carried, or shared by individuals or by societies.

Interstitial Curriculum A label used for that which has been identified as providing the curricular mortar for binding the curricular areas of interaction together.

Metalinguistic A term used to describe the branch of linguistics dealing with relations between language and the other elements of a culture.

Metanarrative This term identifies an abstract idea that is thought to be a comprehensive explanation of historical experience or knowledge. Also, in the theories of structuralism and discourse, it can be called a grand narrative, or overarching narrative, that describes or includes other narratives.

Multinational A term implying that there is one company with offices in many countries. When applied to education, this is not normally the case, but there is potential for this sort of environment to occur, especially in education in an international context.

Nation A term used to demonstrate the cohesiveness of a community that may or may not share one or more commonalities such as geographical location, religious sentiment, cultural traditions, or a common language.

Neostructuralism A term used to denote an attempt to reinvigorate the use of structuralism as a tool for analyzing mass education. The importance of neostructuralism is that it attempts to incorporate a more in-depth approach to a structural analysis.

Pan-national A term used to label organizations that work consciously to reduce tensions and misunderstandings across nations by promoting global initiatives, knowledge and empathy. It may also be thought that nongovernmental organizations found throughout the world are pan-national, or are in the position to be termed as such.

Paradigm A label used to identify certain patterns in an environment that belong exclusively to that environment. In this case, a paradigm often refers to the sociopolitical orientation that is found within the educational environment. These orientations can include hegemonic, accommodating, critical, or transformative practices which usually directly affect the outcome of the student.

Paradigmatic Curriculum A label used to identify the culminating patterns found when the academic, pastoral, and hidden curricular programs have combined to create a distinct learning community.

Postmodern This term is a concept that adopts the attitude that one can do anything at anytime for any reason, and it assumes that the individual or the group take on the responsibility of adopting or creating a set of norms and values that best fit the new perspective. The result is that previous social models (religion, business, ethics, etc.) have now been jeopardized by a different attitude toward life.

Second-order Change A concept used to define a nonlinear progression, a transformation from one state to another. Within the context of education, second order change indicates a shift away from current bureaucratic patterns and traditions to a more organic organization that encourages process oriented, community based interactions and democratic decision making models.

Semiotics A study of patterned human communication behavior accomplished through an analysis of the relevant symbols and signs that are associated with particular areas of society.

Sociohistorical A term used to describe the social and historical influences on a group or community.

Sociopolitical A term used to describe the social and political influences on a group or community.

Structuralism A school of thought common to several of the human sciences that attempt to define phenomena as organized totalities. Several theorists believe the use of studying opposites in nature and in society (e.g., Boy vs. girl, young vs. old, etc.) can help to clarify the environment that is being studied. Some of the theorists include de Saussure, Piaget, and Levi-Strauss.

Supranational A term that offers the concept of transcending national limits to create the appropriate ideological and sociological backdrop for restructuring an institutional environment.

Transformative Intellectual This is an individual who has been granted the opportunity to utilize his intellectual powers to solve problems. He deals critically with issues that bear relevance to immediate or future educational and social situations, and he works to effect transformations in his environment.

Transnational A term used as an alternative descriptor for institutions that promote a mononational culture and who are marketing to a mononational (monocultural) clientele regardless of the actual physical location of the institution.

Reference List

Altrichter, H. et al. *Teachers Investigate Their Work*. London: Routledge, 1993.

Archer, M. S. 1984. *Social Origins of Educational Systems*. London: Sage Publications.

Armitage, P. 1974. *A History of Western Education*. London: Routledge.

Aronowitz, S. and Giroux, H.A. 1993. *Post Modern Education; Politics and Social Change*. Minnesota, USA: University of Minnesota Press.

Appadurai, A. 1990. "Cultural Flows" In *Global Culture: Nationalism, Globalisation and Modernity* edited by Mike Featherstone, 295–310. London: Sage Publications.

Anderson, L. 1979. *Schooling and Citizenship in a Global Age: An Exploration of the Meaning and Significance of Global Education*. Indiana: Indiana University.

Banks, O. 1976. *The Sociology of Education*. London: B.T. Bratsford.

Barthes, R. 1972. *Mythologies*. (Translation by Lavers A) New York: Noonday Press.

Bartlett, J. 1980. *Familiar Quotations*. Boston: Little, Brown and Company.

Bartlett, Kevin. 1996. Articulating the International Curriculum—Part 1: Continuity through Commonality. *International Schools Journal*, 16, 1: 30–38.

Beare, H. and Slaughter, R. 1993. *Education for the Twenty-first Century*. London: Routledge.

Becker, J. M. 1979. *Schooling for a Global Age*. London: McGraw-Hill Book Co.

Bell, J. 1987. *Doing Your Research Project*. Buckingham: Open University Press.

Bennett, S. J. 1974. *The School: An Organisational Analysis*. London: Blackie.

Blenkin, G. M., G. Edwards and A.V. Kelly. 1992. *Change and the Curriculum*. London: Paul Chapman Publishing.

Boulding, E. 1988. *Building a Global Civic Culture: Education for an Interdependent World*. New York: Syracuse University Press.

Bowles, S. & Gintis, H. 1976. *Schooling in Capitalist America*. USA: Basic Books, Harper Collins Publishers.

Brandon, E. P. 2002. *Education as Second Order*. Paper presented at the Annual Conference of the Society for Applied Philosophy, June, at Mansfield College, UK.

Brickman, W. W. 1985. *Educational Roots and Routes in Western Europe*. New Jersey: Emeritus.

Bullock, A. et al. 1988. *The Fontana Dictionary of Modern Thought, 2nd Edition*. Glasgow, UK: Fontana Press.

Calvert, B. 1975. *The Role of The Pupil*. London: Routledge and Kegan Paul.

Carder, Maurice. 1993. Are We Creating Biliterate Bilinguals? ECIS, UK: *International Schools Journal*, Autumn.

Carder, M. *Untitled*, unpublished academic paper

Coggin, P. A. 1979. *Education for the Future—The Case for a Radical Change*. Oxford: Pergamon Press.

Cohen L. and L. Manion. 1989. *Research Methods in Education, Third edition*. London: Routledge.

Coles, K. ed. 1981. *The Future of Education: Policy Issues and Challenges*. Beverly Hills: Sage.

Cook, T. G. ed. 1974. *The History of Education in Europe*. London: Methuen and Company.

Cook, V. 1991. *Second Language Learning and Language Teaching*. London: Edward Arnold.

Coulby, D. and Jones, C. 1995. *Postmodernity and European Education Systems*. London: Trentham Books.

Crossley, M. and Broadfoot, P. 1992. "Comparative and International Research in Education; Scope, Problems, and Potential." *British Educational Research Journal* 18, 2: 99–112.

Davies, L. 1994. "Can Students Make a Difference? International Perspectives on Transformative Education." *International Studies in Sociology of Education*, Volume 4, No 1: 43–56.

De Alba, A. et al. 2000. *Curriculum in the Postmodern Condition*. Oxford: Peter Lang.

Dillard, C. 1993. "Learning Styles from a Multicultural Perspective: Negotiating the Development of Curricula." In *Curriculum Planning: A new Approach, Sixth Edition* edited by Hass, G. and Parkay, F. W. Boston: Allyn and Bacon.

Docherty, T. ed. 1993. *Postmodernism: A Reader*. Cambridge: University Press.

Drennen, Helen. 1997. "Keynote Address" presented at the International Baccalaureate Organization's Regional Conference, October in Lome, Togo.

Durkheim, E. 1977. *The Evoluition of Educational Thought.* London: RKP.

Easton, J. 2002. *Personal Letter from the offices of the Qualifications Curriculum Authority Customer Services Represenative.* QCA.

Edwards, A. M. 1996. *Educational Theory as Political Theory.* Aldershot UK: Avebury.

Ellwood, C. 1996. *The Matter of Values.* International Schools Journal, 16,1: 39–45.

Emory, W. C. 1980. *Business Research Methods.* USA: Richard D. Irwin.

Epstein. R. 2007. *The Case Against Adolescence: Rediscovering the Adult in Every Teen.* Sanger, California: Word Dancer Press.

European Council of International Schools.1998. *The International Schools Directory 1998/99.* Petersfield: ECIS.

Featherstone, M. 1983. *Global Culture: Nationalism, Globalization, and Modernity.* London: Sage Publications.

Feldman, D. H. 1980. *Beyond Universals in Cognitive Development.* New Jersey: Ablex Publishing Corporation.

Fennes, H. and K. Hapgood. 1997. *Intercultural Learning in the Classroom.* London: Cassell.

Findlay, R. 1997. *International Education Handbook.* London: Kogan Page.

Fraenkel, J. and Wallen, N. 1993. *How to Design and Evaluate Research in Education.* New York: McGraw-Hill.

Franklin, B. M. 1986. *Building the American Community: The School Curriculum and the Search for Social Control.* Lewes, USA: Falmer Press.

Freire, Paolo. 1990. *The Pedagogy of the Oppressed, 32nd Printing.* New York: Continuum.

Fullan, Michael. 2003. *Change Forces with a Vengeance*. New York: Routledge Falmer.

Gammage, P. 1971. *Teacher and Pupil*. London: Vegan & Routledge.

Gedge, Joseph L.1991. *The Hegemonic Curriculum and School Dropout: The Newfoundland Case*. Journal of Education Policy 6, 2: 215–224.

Gellar, C. 1981. *International Education: Some Thoughts on What It Is and What It Might Be*. International Schools Journal, 1, 1: 21–26.

Gibson, R. 1984. *Strucuralism and Education*. London: Hodder and Stoughton.

Giroux, H. 1992. *Border Crossings, Cultural Workers, and the Politics of Education*. London: Routledge.

Golby, M. and Greenwald, J. eds. 1975. *Curriculum Design*. London: Croom Helm.

Gollnick, D. M. and P C Chinn. 1990. *Multicultural Education in a Pluralistic Society* London: Merrill.

Grant, C. 1985. "Schools That Make an Imprint: Creating a Strong Positive Ethos" in *The Challenge to American Schools*, ed. John Bunzel, Oxford: Oxford University Press.

Green, A. 1997. *Education, Globalisation and the Nation State*. London: Macmillan.

Hall, G. E. and S. E. Loucks. 1978. Innovation Configurations: Analyzing the Adaptation of Innovations. In Marzano, R.J. 1995. *A New Paradigm for Educational Change*. Proquest Information and Learning Company, Winter 1995. (http://findarticles.com/p/articles/mi_qa3673/is_199501/ai_n8730397/pg_1)

Hargreaves, A. 2009 *The Fourth Way*. Corwin: USA.

Harrison, L. E. and S P Huntington. eds. 2000. *Culture Matters: How Values Shape Human Progress*. New York: Basic Books.

Hass, G. & F. W. Parkay. 1993. *Curriculum Planning: A New Approach, sixth edition*. London: Allyn and Bacon.

Hayden, M. and Jeff Thompson. 1995a. *International Schools and International Education: a Relationship Reviewed*. Oxford Review of Education, 21, 3: 327–345.

Hayden, M. and Jeff Thompson. 1995b. *Perceptions of International Education: A Preliminary Study*. International Review of Education 41,5: 389-404.

Hayden, M. and Jeff Thompson. 1996. *Potential Difference: The Driving Force for International Education*. International Schools Journal 16, 1: 46–57.

Hayden, M. and Jeff Thompson. 1997. *Student Perspectives on International Education: A European Dimension*. Oxford Review of Education 23, 4.

Hayden, M. and C. S. D. Wong. 1997. *The International Baccalaureate: International Education and Cultural Preservation*. Educational Studies 23, 3.

Hayden, M. and Jeff Thompson. eds. 1998. *International Education; Principles and Practice* London, Kogan Page.

Hazelwood, R. D. 1990. *Attitudes on Performance Indicators* in *Performance Indicators, Bera Dialogues 2*. ed. Fitzgibbon, C. T. Clevedon: Multilingual Matters.

Held, D. 1999. *Global Transformations, Politics, Economics, and Culture* Cambridge: Polity Press.

Hicks, D. and C. Holden. 1995. *Visions of the Future*. London: Trentham Books.

Hicks, D. ed. 1994. *Preparing for the Future*. London: Adamantine Press Ltd.

Hirst, P. H. and R. S. Peters. 1970. *The Logic of Education*. London: Routledge & Kegan Paul.

Hofstede, G. 1994. *Cultures and Organizations: Software of the Mind: Intercultural Cooperation and its Importance for Survival.* London: Harper Collins.

Holmes, M. and E A Wynne. 1989. *Making the School an Effective Community: Belief, Practice and Theory in School Administration.* New York: Falmer Press.

Howard, K. and J. Peters. 1990. *Managing Management Research.* United Kingdom: MCB University Press.

IGCSE. January, *The IGCSE Guidelines News, Issue 14, 1993.* London: IGCSE.

International Baccalaureate Organization. May 1997. *Examiners Report.* Cardiff, IBO.

International Baccalaureate Organization. February 2001. *IB Public Prospectus Information.* Cardiff: IBO.

James, P. 1997. "Transformative learning: Promoting Change across Cultural Worlds." *Journal of Vocational Education and Training,* 49, 2.

A. Jefferson and D. Robey. eds. 1982. *Modern Literary Theory.* London: Batsford Academic and Educational.

Johansen, L. 1978. *Lectures on Macroeconomic Planning: Centralization, Decentralization, Planning Under Uncertainty.* Oxford: North Holland Publishing.

Jones, P. W. 1997. "On World Bank Education Financing." *Comparative Education* 33, 1: 117–130.

Jonietz, P. L. and N.D.C. Harris. Eds. 1991. *World Yearbook of Education 1991: International Schools and International Education.* London: Kogan Page.

Keohane, R. O. and J. S. Nye. Eds. 1971. *Transnational Relations and World Politics.* London: Cambridge, Mass; Harvard University Press.

Klein, G. Ed. 1982. *Multicultural Teaching for Practitioners in School and Community.* New Jersey, Trent Book.

Kueng, H. 1998. *A Global Ethic for Global Politics and Economics.* Oxford: Oxford University Press.

Kingdon, M. 1991. *The Reform of the Advanced Level.* London: Hodder and Staughton.

Lane, M. Ed. 1970. *Structuralism: a Reader.* London: Jonathan Cape.

Lang, P. H. 1963. *Music in Western Civilization.* London: J. M. Dent and Sons.

Langford, M. 1998. Global Nomads, Third Culture Kids and International Schools in Hayden M & Jeff Thompson. eds. 1998. *International Education: Principles and Practice.* London: Kogan Page.

Lawton, D. 1975. *Class, Culture, and the Curriculum.* London: Routledge & Kegan Paul.

Lawton, D. et al. 1978. *Theory and Practice of Curriculum Studies.* London: Routledge & Kegan Paul.

Leach, R. J. 1969. *International Schools and Their Role in International Education.* London: Pergamon Press.

Lechte, J. ed. 1994 *Fifty Key Contemporary Thinkers.* London: Routledge.

Lewis, C. W. 1994. *The Case for the AP.* New York: The College Entrance Examination Board.

Lewy, A. ed. 1991. *The International Encyclopedia of Curriculum.* Oxford: Pergamon Press.

Maier, H. 1987. *Developmental Group Care of Children and Youth: Concepts and Practice.* New York: Haworth.

Mallinson, V. 1975. *An Introduction to the Study of Comparative Education 4th Edition.* UK: Heinemann Educational Books Ltd.

Marland, M. 1980. *The Comprehensive School: Organization and Responsibility.* London: National Book League, Wandsworth.

Martin, J. R. 1994. *Changing the Educational Landscape*. London: Routledge.

Mattern, G. 1988. *Meteorology and the International School: Unsettled Days Ahead, Followed by Better Weather—Maybe*. International Schools Journal, 16: 7-14.

Matthews, M. 1988. *The Ethos of International Schools*. University of Oxford, MSc Thesis.

Marsh, C.J. 1992. *Key Concepts for Understanding Curriculum*. London: Falmer Press.

McCormick, R. and James, M. 1990. *Curriculum Evaluation in Schools, Second Edition*. London: Routledge.

McKenzie, M. 1998. "Going, Going, Gone...Global!" in *International Education; Principles and Practice* ed. Mary Hayden and Jeff Thompson. London: Kogan Page.

McLeish, K. ed. 1995. *Key Ideas in Human Thought*. California: Prima Publishing.

Mortimer, J. and P. Mortimer. 1986. *Secondary School Examinations*. London: Bedford Way Papers 18, Institute of Education, University of London.

Neville, M. 1995. School Culture and Effectiveness in an Asian Pluralistic Society *International Studies in Educational Administration*. 23, 2: 28-37.

Nicholas, E. J. 1983. *Issues in Education: A Comparative Analysis*. London: Harper& Row Publishers.

Nixon, J. 1992. *Evaluating the Whole Curriculum*. Philadelphia: Open University Press, USA.

Onions, C. T. 1966. *The Oxford Dictionary of Etymology*. Oxford: Clarendon Press.

Ontario Ministry of Education. 1987. *Curriculum Guidelines for English*. MOE: Ontario, Canada.

Oppenheim, A. N. 1992. *Questionnaire Design, Interviewing and Attitude Measurement, new edition.* London: Pinter.

Ornstein, A. C. 1989. *Emerging Curriculum Trends: An Agenda for the Future. In: Curriculum Planning: A New Approach, sixth edition* Boston: Allyn and Baker.

Parkay, F. W. 1993. "Curriculum Reform: Past and Present." In: *Curriculum Planning: A New Approach, sixth edition.* Boston: Allyn and Baker.

Pearce, R. 1994. "International Schools: the Multinational Enterprises' Best Friends." *CBI Relocation News.* 32: 8-9.

Peters, R. S. ed. 1973. *Philosophy of Education.* Oxford: Oxford University Press.

Phenix, H. P. 1964. *Realms of Meaning: a Philosophy for the Curriculum for General Education.* London: McGraw-Hill.

Piaget, J. 1971. *Structuralism.* London: Routledge and Kegan Paul.

Pike, G. and D. Selby. 1988. *Global Teacher, Global Learner* Toronto: Hodder and Stoughton, York University Press.

Pratt, D. 1980. *Curriculum Design and Development.* London: Harcourt Brace Jovanovich.

Proctor, P. ed. 1987. *Longman Dictionary of Contemporary English.* London: Longman.

Rea-Dickins, P. and K. Germaine.1992. *Evaluation* Oxford: Oxford University Press.

Sampson, D. and H. Smith. 1957. "A Scale to Measure World-minded Attitudes." *Journal of Social Psychology,* 45: 99-106.

Sapsford, R. and W. Jupp. Eds. 1986. *Data Collection and Analysis.* London: Sage Publications.

Sarup, M. 1993. *Post-Structuralism and Post-Modernism 2nd edition* London: Harvester Wheatsheaf.

Schein, E. H. 1992. *Organisational Culture and Leadership, Second Edition.* San Francisco: Josey-Bass.

Shor, I. 1986. "Equality is Excellence: Transforming Teacher Education and the Learning Process." *Harvard Education Review,* 56.

Short, E. 1971. *Education in a Changing World.* Oxford: Alden & Mowbray Ltd.

Silverman, H. J. 1997. *Inscriptions; After Phenomenology and Structuralism.* USA: Northwestern University Press.

Skilbeck, M. ed. 1980. *Evaluating the Curriculum in the Eighties.* London: Hodder and Stoughton.

Slattery, P. 1995. *Curriculum Development in the Postmodern Era.* London: Garland Publishing.

Slaughter, R. A. 1985. "The Dinosaur and the Dream: Rethinking Education for the Future." *World Studies Journal,* 6, 1: 2–5.

Spaulding, S., J. Colcucci and J. Flint. 1982. *International Education, Encyclopedia on Educational Research,* Vol. 2. USA: Thea.

Spring, J. 1998. *Education and the Rise of the Global Economy.* New Jersey: Laurence Erlbaum Associates.

Sturrock, M. ed. 1979. *Structuralism and Since; From Levi-Strauss to Derrida,* Oxford: Oxford University Press.

Sylvester, R. 2000. "The Unintended Classroom: Changing the Angle of Vision on International Education." *International Schools Journal.* XIX, No. 2: 20–28.

Tayeb, M. H. 1996. *The Management of a Multicultural Workforce.* Chichester, UK: John Wiley & Sons.

Thompson, D. 1995. *The Concise Oxford Dictionary of Current English,* 9th edition Oxford, Clarendon Press.

Tompkins, J. P. ed. 1980. *Reader Respose Criticism: From Formalism to Post-Structuralism.* USA: Johns Hopkins University Press.

Trompenaars, F. 1993. *Riding the Waves of Culture*. London: Nicholas Brealey Publishing.

Tyler, R. W. 1949. *Basic Principles of Curriculum and Instruction*. London: University of Chicago Press.

UNESCO. 1968. *Guiding Principles Relating to Education for International Understanding*. Recommendation No. 64 adopted by the International Conference on Public Education at its 31st session.

Usher, R. and R. Edwards. 1994. *Postmodernism and Education*. London: Routledge.

UK Dept.of Education. *The School and the Community* UK: Department of Education.

Vyas, K. C. 1983. *UNESCO Projects on International Understanding and Peace*. Bombay, Somaiya Publications.

Walker, D. F. 1971. "A Nationalistic Model for Curriculum Development." *School Review*, 80,1: 55–61.

Wallace, E. ed. (1997) *The IB Hexagon: Straitjacket or Flexible Model for the Future?* Cardiff: IB World, April edition.

Warnock, M. 1977. *Schools of Thought*. London: Faber and Faber.

Waters, T., R. J. Marzano, and B. McNulty. 2003. *Balanced Leadership: What 30 Years of Research Tells Us About the Effect of Leadership on Student Achievement*. McRel. http://www.mcrel.org/PDF/LeadershipOrganizationDevelopment/5031RR_BalancedLeadership.pdf

Waters, T. and S. Grubb. 2004. *The Leadership We Need: Using Research to Strengthen the Use of Standards for Administrator Preparation and Licensure Programs*. McRel. http://www.mcrel.org/PDF/LeadershipOrganizationDevelopment/4005PI_leadership_we_need.pdf

Weatherall, M. et al. 2001. *Discourse Theory and Practice*. London: Sage Publications

Willis, D. and W. Enloe. 1990. "Lessons of International Schools: Global Education in the 1990's *the Educational Forum*." 54,(2): 169–83.

Peter J. Zsebik, Ph.D.

Zsebik, P. 2000. The Politics of International Education In Hayden, M, and Jeff Thompson. *International Schools and International Education: Improving Teaching, Management and Quality.* London: Kogan Page.

Zsebik, P. 2003. *A Comparative Analysis of Four Approaches to Curriculum Offered in International Schools.* PhD Diss., University of Bath, UK.

Zsebik, P. 2007. *Toward Understanding the Role of Emotional Intelligence in the Academic Classroom.* Paper presented at the Annual Quest Conference for Educators, November 15–18, in Toronto, Canada.

Zsebik, P. 2008. *First- and Second-order Change in Education and Its Implications for Future Directions.* Paper presented at the Canadian Society for Studies in Education, May 15–18, in Ottawa, Canada.

INDEX

Page numbers in *italics* refer to figures.

C